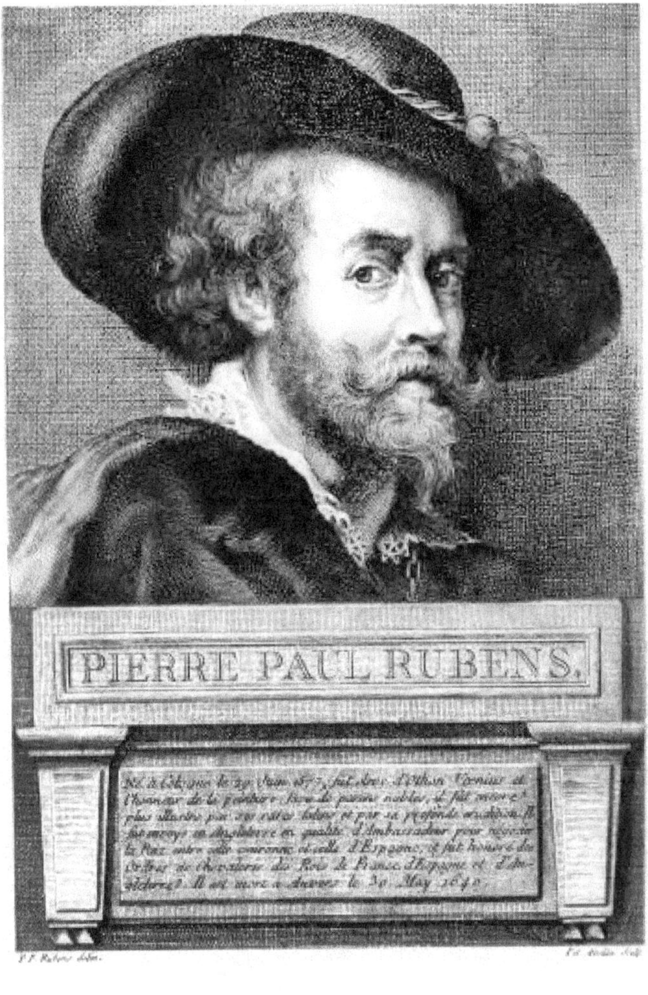

PIERRE PAUL RUBENS.

Né à Cologne le 29 Juin 1577, fut élève d'Othon Vénius et l'honneur de la peinture, être les peintres nobles, il fut même plus illustre par son esprit si poli, se par sa profonde érudition. Il fut envoyé en Angleterre en qualité d'Ambassadeur pour négocier la Paix, entre cette couronne, et celle d'Espagne, et fut honoré de l'Ordre de Chevalerie des Rois de France, d'Espagne et d'Angleterre. Il est mort à Anvers le 30 May 1640.

P.P. Rubens delin.   Ed. Scoten sculp.

Theory of the Figure Human

=====================================

Theory of the Figure Human, considers in his Principles, Either in repose or in movement.

Publication translated from Latin by Pierre-Paul Rubens, with XLIV Diagrams engraved by Pierre Aveline, of afterwards the design from this celebrated Artist.

=====================================

What composition limbs, what physical structure outlines, what figure, what specie, human can be beautiful? All animals form closeness man figure. Cicero, of natural Decorum, Book I.

A Paris, street Dauphipne,

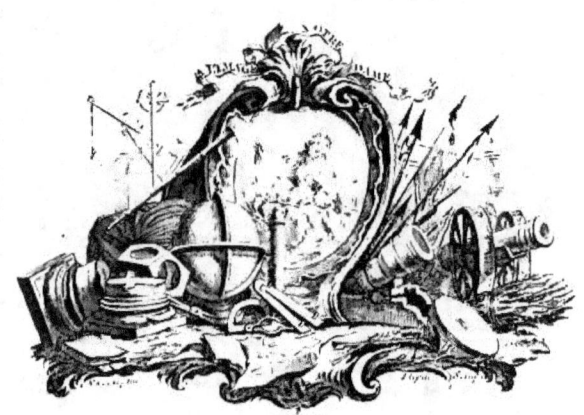

Among Charles-Antoine Jombert, Father, Library of the Artillery and of the Genius.
M. DCC. LXXIII.
With approval and privilege from King.
17th Century rewritten 20th

ISBN-13: 978-1530484560

ISBN-10: 1530484561

Warning
From Library.

The translation from this publication from Rubens level proportions from the figure human-size, what I present to the Public, debit volume existence at the purchase what I have done at the sales of the flower Huquier, around the fine from the year last, some boards from cooper of after the design trace of the main of Rubens to the intelligence of volume manuscript. To the advance sheets from those boards was combine one copy from speech in Latin, with his translation in French; although it was if poorly apex, if gravid from against direction, and if little conform to the original, that it myself have to here renounce, and me determine at in about it do personally same one tidings traditions of after of Rubens.

Somebody be perhaps amazed what this work who to done so much from interference among the amateurs, and who was considerations since long time by the artist with one species of impatience, respond if not much to the upper class that the somebody about it have conceived, and to the grand reputation from volume Author, who was scholar and very laying in the letters, and who possessing uppermost the talent from the paint. Although somebody debit do attention what this manuscript not at never prime compose by Rubens in the intention from him do see the day; it was only a *repertoire* in which he accommodation by penned, for his proper to instruction, the precept and the consciousness that it agreed, either in the nature, either in the difference Authors whose the make the reading, instead of ornament his memory from this that it here find from more remarkable.

Yet, like all this who see of one grand artist debit be precious for the ones who rest the same quarry, I me am determine to make part to the Public from those fragments some studies from Rubens, such what I the calling found in volume Manuscript. I about it am only embanked two arrange in chapters from principles ballistics; the one level the proprieties some numbers apply to the operations from chemistry; the another rate the formation primitive from the man set up from manner hermaphrodite, then divided about it two sexes; level the marriage from sun with the moon; and suchlike reveries long haul from the philosophe abstruse, who mid have appear unintelligible and without suite, and who well from elsewhere too foreigner to the subject principal, who pointless and absurdist.

With remainder, Rubens doesn't matter not the alone grand artist who self either shrewd from unite the principles from design with the mysteries from the chemistry and the reverie from the astrology judicial. The subtle universal joint (gimbal), Albert Durer, and Jean-Paul Lomazze, who have penned level the proportions from the figure human, in this way what Vincent Scamozzi, and Juste Aurele Meyssonier, in their idea from one architecture universal, are fallen in the same space, and oneself are in the same way mislay in the labyrinth obscure some terms from the chemistry and from the philosophy satiric implicated with those from design. We not about it give in order to proof what the three extract according to from draft from Proportions from Jean – Paul Lomazze, translated from the Italian by Hilaire Pader, Peintre Tolosain, in-folio form to Toulouse in 1649.

"these grand proportions harmonics what Lomazze done come across in the body human according to the numbers and the tonal from the music, testify the perfect symmetry from this small world; this be reason the man be agreed the more perfect overture of the nature, the image of Creator, and the King some animals, who contain inside oneself the four elements. From strength what not only the music there found the division from its tonal, the geometric its points, lines, and figures, although from moreover the astrology here come across its star, the philosophy his discipline and its form, and the chemistry the difference from its naval vessels and furnaces. And not to you amazed not if I mixed here the chemistry, because I thy assure what if you not be satiric, you not become not excellent Painter". Discourse from Pader, are the end from chapter VI, page 22 of the work estate above.

"From more, the vessel, baroque (poetic), galleys, and similar, well noble from bodies human, to the example from the ark from Noah: that the be agreed that same teach from make the ark to Noah, just like the one who have sagely built the machine of the world, all the perfections from which it have epilog to the plus high degree of them man, from whereabouts the one be known as grand and the another small world. This be why those who are measure that little world, have divided the body in six feet, and the feet in ten degrees, and the degree in five minutes, who make the number from sixty degrees, or from three one hundred, minutes, to whom they paragon as much as from cubit geometries, by the which the ark from Noah be familiar with described by Moyse. For like the body human to three hundred minutes from long, fifty from large, and thirty from tall, in this way the ark barrel from three one hundred cubits from long, fifty from wide. and thirty from height J.P. Lomazze, from the proportion. Chapter. XXX, page 83, gran edition.

The ruler some proportions to prime observation by the more excellent and illustrate Painter who have prime the splendor and the light from our time, and have ensure and testy the excellence from proportions from seven governors from planet, enter which the first, without exception, to Michel Ange Buonarotte; and beyond him, the price from former the bodies venereal, in other words by the proportion from Venus, known given to the grand Painter Raphael Sancio of Urbin: some solar, to Leonardo from Vinci, Florentine: some Marital, to Polidore from Caravagge: some Price, with Andre Manteigne, Mantouan: some fanciful, with Titian Veccelli, from Cadore, and in last place some jovial, with Gaudens Ferrare from Valdusie, Milanois". Ibidem. Chapter XXXI, page 88.

One not arguable better finish this Warning what by the extract following from the Preface stake belong to the expression from school of Uranie, by M. from Querlon, Author much valued and reputed by the excellent work periodical whose the enrich since long terms the republic from literature: this extract proved evidently what the work what the one order on this day to the Public be known and desire for long term by the amateurs and the decree, like one as ordered remarkable heretofore.

"Rubens, genius himself poetic, and from more steep from Otto Van Veen, who have so much from flavor for the poetry, to foreshore a monument from studies so he possess make from afterwards the poets, in a collection where to be outcome the most from actions of the man, in compliance with to the description that in have make the ancient Authors The include one development from selection extracts principles from Virgil, and who are like as much as from frames from combats, from shipwreck, from plot, and from mortician: this so it have huddled so much to volume usage, what for compare to the painting from Raphael and from another schoolteacher who before treatise the same subject.

The proud to hope what this repertory known between the hand of all the Painters; although he dexterous again better what each person, disloyal his type and his taste, tart self-form oneself one all one poetic. Rubens have if well understood the need what the more well off imagination to from be sustained for the lecture, what matching, about it painting, it himself utter read or selection from history, or some poetry.

Leonard from Vinci, long-term earlier than Rubens, have done some extract to little close to similar, where he powerful ideas poetic, subject from composition, character, and all the features from erudition that he was pass in his frames ". Preface from the School from Uranie, page xvi and suiv.

To the relic, somebody pray the Lecture from observation what this not be point here a Treaties elementary rate the design, in which one somebody himself either propose from developer all of the principal from that art, although what this are some reflection particular from Rubens rate the different character from body from the man and from the female, occasion by the lectures from Virgil, from Pline, and from some other Author ancient. For the compensate from this who lack to this work, somebody order in a second volume, who mounting from supplement to this one, the principal from design apply to the practical, followed from one grand quantity of example from all the parties from body human, from diverse figure from Academic, and from a lot from another swindle from after the best master from our School Francoise modern. Those two volumes appear in same time, and self-vend ensemble or separately, for the convenience from Amateurs.

Various extracts of the history natural of Pline, on the statues of ancients.

Table
Some Chapters and Articles.

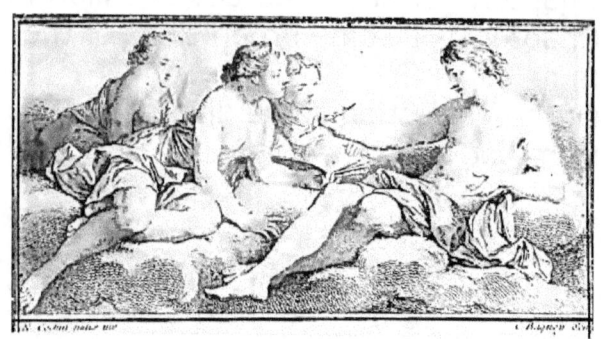

Theory of the figure Human.

Chapter First

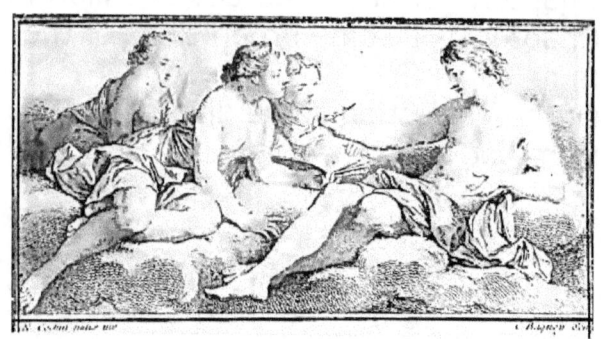ne can reduce the elements or principles of the figure human, to the cube, to the circle, and to the triangle.

For shape a cube, it almost commences by describe a quarry, which being himself compose from four parties, be necessaire engendered of a number; for one is one, and abode always one so much that it is alone: it can so be considered like one point.

Two, or the number binary, the more little some number who express several unites, is the element of the line. The line multiply product one surface: the simpler of these figures is the triangle, proceed from number ternary. The is compose of the three lines plumb, who self-combine through their extremities. The quart just afterward: it at for elements four lines plumb equally separate the one from the other in all their points, and who oneself affect by the extremities. From this assemblage appear the rectangle solid, called substance or matter. Because having posture four points equally distance the one from the other, if somebody the joined the one to the other through from lines straight, they product the base from cube who in support through the parities and the ribbing dispose to equal height, through the means from four lines raise perpendicularly level the angles from that base. Now, the cube are six ribbing is with: a level which itself support: one another ribbing about it top opposite at the base: and four other who shape volume contours: similar is one from at preform.

This cube or quart perfect is the element primitive (1) from all the bodies strong and vigorous, such that the Hero, the Athletes, and from all this who debit express from the simplicity, from the weight, from the firmness, and from the force; because the cube at one base level which one it can self-support without no aid foreign, and it conserve one empire universal level the body human, rate-all in the type masculine. In the female, to the contrary, the force from her angles is weakened and diminished in form of sphere.

(1) E.g. cube, five figure ab all sides square, is all male, or manly, and whatever serious, strength, robust, compacted, and athleticisms is: and whatever form foursquare eliminate, amplitudes too cut off. Quintile. Book I, Chapter. X.

Some three species of gender parity types and robust.

We well, by the statues antiques, what the Greeks distinction three sort of bodies strong and vigorous. We have an example from the first species in the statue of Hercules, work perfect in all its points, and who characterized the more grand strength. Glycon, Athenian, is the author from this masterpiece from sculpture who self it to Rome in the courtyard from palace Farnese. Like the strength from this demigod have to surpass all this let somebody perhaps imagine from more kind, the Sculptor to employ in that figure supernatural this who designated the more this character in the lion, the bull, and the horse. That is this let somebody sees clearly in the felt from Hercules, who have one resemblance perfect with the mane of lion or of bull: it in is from same from almost through his head who attaches of bull: the front at something of the bull and of the lion: the bun of the saddle and volume fitting level the assist are fleshy and plump from muscles like those from bull. See the boards (diagrams draws) I, II, III, and IV, and mostly the draw V.

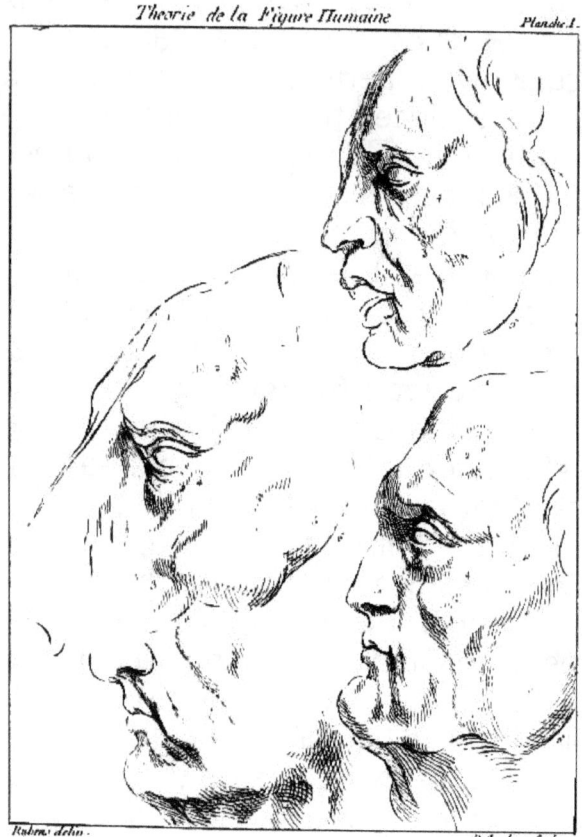

Theorie de la Figure Humaine

Planche.1.

Rubens delin.

P.Avelne Sculps.

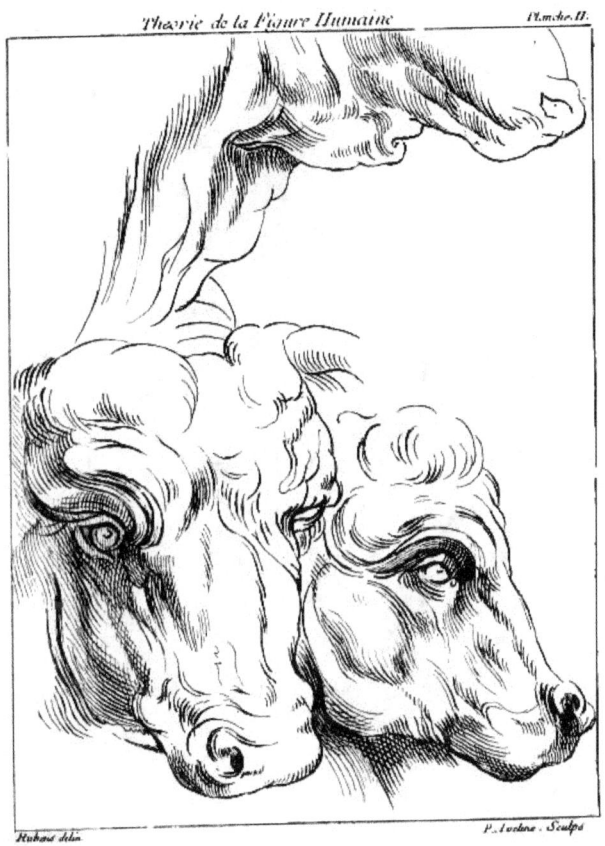

Rubens delin.   P. Aveline. Sculps.

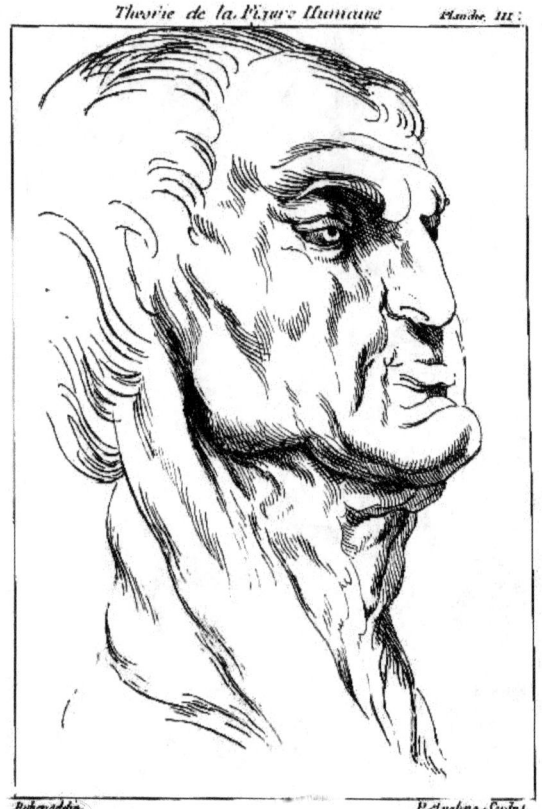

Rubens delin.   P. Aveline Sculps.

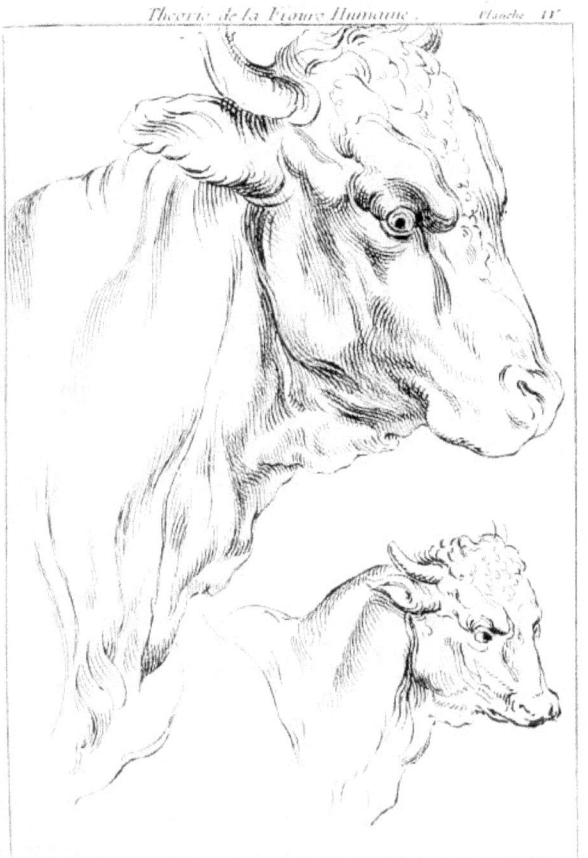

Rubens delin.   P. Aveline Sculp.

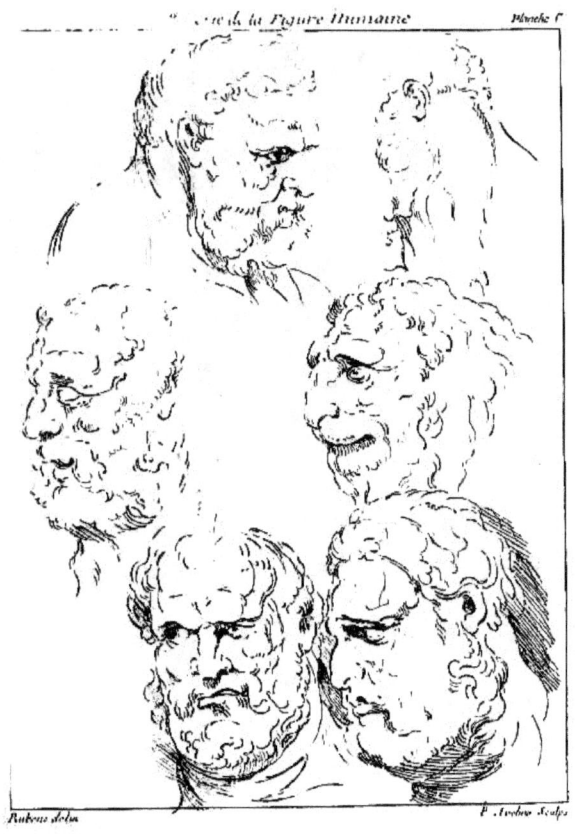

Rubens delin   P. Avelines Sculps

Somebody sees again to Rome, among the antiques, one other statue of Hercules of one dimensions more elegant, and less thick. His chest is more steep, his shoulder are more broad-brimmed, his arm are more stretched out, his hands more grand; the muscles from stomach more close and more narrowed; the hip bone is protruding; his cuffs are of one belle thickness and of one form irreprehensible, energetic in belittle throughout length from feet; the heel a little grand. All the extremities from limbs with this figure diversion more smallness to measure that it is elongated from trunk, to the imitation of one pyramid who be the element primitive from extremities from bodies human.

In that identical figure the muscles are treaty with a lot of art and of elegance; similar to with petites rise who one looming to the middle of one valley by their breadth and their projection, they are be able to see the force from bodies the more vigorous combine to the beauty with forms and to observation exact from rules prescribed by the master from the art the more experience.

The Ethiopians, The Africans, and the Turks disciple in some manner from proportions from that statue: not that it have the some force, but their limb are too little near close similar to those from that Hercules. They have, for example, the head round, the hair frizzy like the fur from bull, the collar short and full from muscles, the cuff broad, etc. To See the drawing (boards) V and VI.

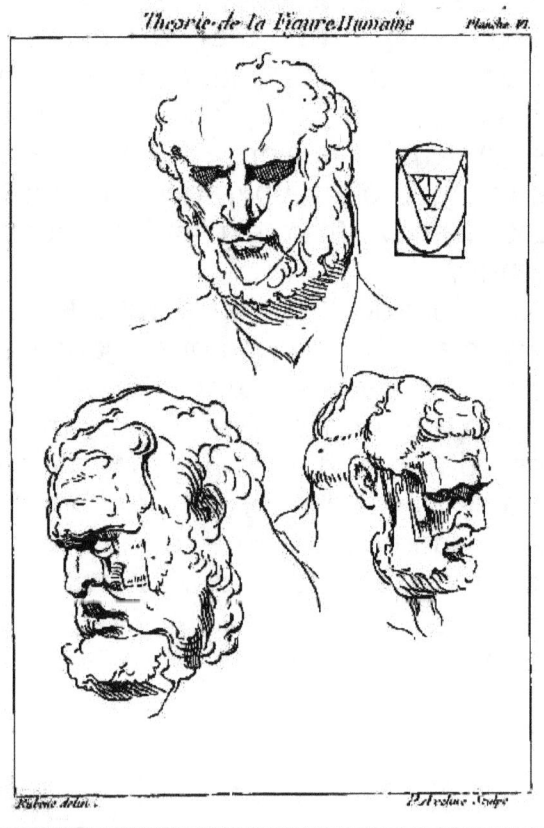

Theorie de la Figure Humaine   Planche VI

Rubens delin.   P. Avoine Sculp.

In the second species from bodies robust, the muscles not are pace one visible, but the figure is more fleshy; inkind that the limb at parish almost too grand, the nerve (courage) being everywhere cover from flesh. The antiquity we in offer an example perfect in the figure from Nile, and in that one from the Emperor Chest of Drawers represent beneath the figure of Hercules; although in particular in the Nile. Those two sumptuous statues themselves indeed to Rome, in the garden of Vatican.

The third species from body vigorous is more spire, the bone in are more grand, the head more long; the arms, the cuff and the legs well more extend; the stomach is more flat and more narrowed; and the flesh is so much taut everywhere the body what the nerves parish, and what, similar to some strings, somebody the glimpse from side and from other under the skin. The natural would be necessary not nevertheless what that know projected to the excess, neither what that offend the elegance that it is difficult of here observer, to cause some proportions regularly what we be oblige from follow exactly: as to not much what one the neglected, we grave soon in the deformity.

We have a very beautiful shaped from that form elegant, to Rome, in the village Borghese: that is the statue of the Gladiator, who all of the time gate the influence at sound opponent and who shapely oneself guarantee from the one who the menace. That figure is from Theophane (Theophany), of Ephese (Ephebe): it is very beautiful to see from all the ribbing. From those three variety differentness from proportions, we in accessible former one infinity of other whose we all-seeing from all parts some example antiques to Rome, in the palace, the great one for some particular, the district (suburb), the vineyard, the garden, etc. The here at one other strength from figure who not seems steps if appropriate that the one of Hercules for the effort who demand from the force, support nevertheless have the fault from appear weak; although who is holding the middle between those two character. We not may themselves form any idea from the beauty and from the perfection of this nature particular of after the figures human; the Painter and the Sculptor have, for in this way state, built up this genre of beauty as the principle same of their art: that is the character what the ancient Payens (Pagans) gave to their Jupiter, and that our Artists modern have gave to Jesus- Christ. Whatever these figures can appear in whole their parties, they are however so much dispose in their proportion, that we not there acknowledge nothing who there is proper. We of sees a few examples ancient to Rome, such that a few statues of Jupiter and of Mercury, in this way that the ones of Apollo and Antonius, in the garden of Vatican. We some abandoned as well an example modern in the figure of Christ who self-have to Rome, in the temple of the Minerve: work of celebrity Michel-Ange Buonarotti. There all this what I had to say as the cube.

Of circle and of globe.

The circle is the second element primitive of bodies human: it pinched its origin from the unity, that is to say, of point which is his center, which product the circle in the surfaces, and the bowl in the bodies; the unity and the simplicity constitute its existence. That is of this circle or of globe perfect that derive all this who regard the female, or all this who is round, flexible, twisted, curve, etc. (1)

(1) From this circular, five globe perfect, fit all female and womanish, and whatever fleshy, torsos, inflected, twist, curvature, and crooked etc. This form any negate pivot beautiful Plato. Pica (Cicero), from universe Of the Gods, Book I.

as the elevation of back, the thickness from parts superiors of body, such that the chest and the shoulders; and it of the parts inferior, as the belly, the buttocks, all this that is fleshy and muscular, and all the contours external and internal, so such convex than concave. The circle contributes likewise to the formation of the muscles which make move the eyebrows, and that are failing as the forehead; at that of the nose aquiline; and the roundness of the eyes, without that it himself find none muscle falling by above, or none fold to the skin in this place; at the beard of the jaws who if extends in width and that form a circle author of the face. The figure of circle presides also in hair bun of collar, which is very fleshy, so that at the fitting of the shoulders, and at the head entire, the throat under the chin, that is fleshy and surrounded of beard thick, and a one infinity of others parts who have the circle for principle.

Of triangle and from the pyramid. The triangle, third element primitive from bodies human, drawn his origin of number ternary, because it is composing of three lines. In effect, having dispose three points of manner they are equally distant the one of other, and the having joints by as much of lines straight, it in results one form triangular who is the base of the pyramid. The triangle is so the element of the figure in the surface flat, as the pyramid in the solid. The pyramid is one figure solid, who of one surface plane itself high in manner of done the point is called cone or summit. We give the name of base to the part inferior of this figure, whence itself high sparsely to little the grandeur of the pyramid, whose the lines incline in manner of one cone format one pyramid contained in the contour of three ribbing equal. Because, as one base triangular, if the we high three lines straight who himself join the summit, they have to necessarily produce three triangles who constitute the pyramid. This figure dominated as all the parts of the figure human, as we shall see in the examples thereafter; because it given the front all its width, to the temples their fullness, at the act their decrease by the low, to the eye their distance, the nose his parts superior who proceed in decreasing towards the mouth. The triangle given to the shoulders this extended by the top of bodies, format one parallel figure, whose the point resulting the belly button. Finally it presided to the width of all the parts of bodies, so superior being inferior, such that the narrowing of belly by in low, the width of the thigh who proceed in decreasing until foot, as one pyramid, so that the shoulders, the arms, the hands, and the finger who decrease always of more in more. In a word, the globe, or the circle is the element of the head; the cube that of trunk, and the pyramid is the element of the arms and the legs.

Chapter II.

Of the composition of the figure human.

The form virile is the real perfection of the figure human. The idea perfect of the beauty is the work immediate of the Divinity, who the at created unique and of aftermath his proper principles. As though the not in to form of manner that one alone the 2nd, the 3rd the 4th, and all the others creatures that came afterwards, himself make outlying of more in more of this first output of the hands of Creator, and its hold degenerate of his excellency primitive. So changing of form and of character, they have borrowed various parts of lion, of bull, and of horse, who outperform all the other animals by the force, the courage, and the grandeur of bodies. The examples who follow demonstrate the rapport that the figure of the man may to have with these animals.

The cube and the square preform, as they it to previously said, them elements primitive of all this who to of the extended in the bodies human. The triangle and the pyramid there president since the shoulders up to the sole of the feet, so that they the at remark heretofore, in speaking of the proportion elementary.

We see in effect that, in the figure human, all the parts superior are more ample and more breadth, and that they end in decreasing towards the extremities. So the form pyramidal dominated in the figure of the man, and of the cubic in his movements; because this not is pitch the same principle who presided to his actions and the forms of her figure, as we it proves following after in the examples who accompany the description of bodies female.

Of report from the head of the man with that of a few animals.

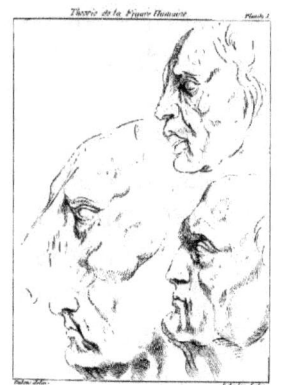

The face of the man is holding a lot of the head of horse; this resemblance is visible in the head of Jules Cesar, and as the board I, or the we may remark as the face who is holding of horse must be long and oval, with the nose long and straight, the bones strongly fancy, the face tough, the act of same, in keeping yet something of more soft and more delicate.

Explanation from the plate I.
1. The advancement of the head.
2. The hollow (sunken) of the head.
3. The emaciation of the jowl (cheek).
4. The bulge of the jowl.
5. The equability or the dish (flat) of the jowl.
6. The part circular of beneath of the head.

The plates II, III and IV. Make one

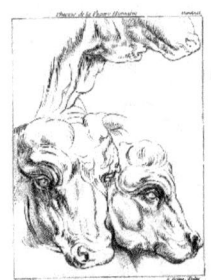 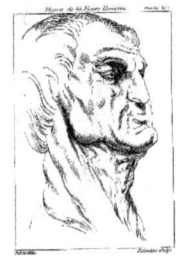 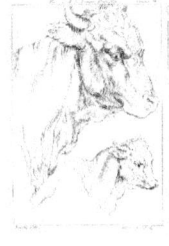

confirmation of the principles established heretofore, and make see the resemblance of face of the man with the head of ox or of bull.

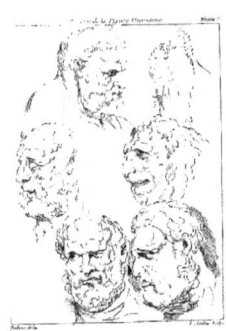

The plate V fact see how the head of Hercules, and that of the Athletes, or that of men the more vigorous, be formed of that of lion, but with so of art and of mellowing that we to of the sentence to himself in descry.

We see as the plate VI, that the man

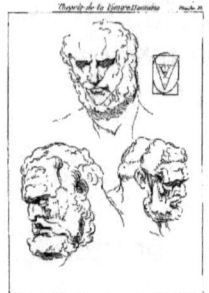

composes of the elements of the universe, participate of all the animals; but the traits that in derive from make if good hearth and so much dispose that we not can them distinguish, as we just of it said. This himself found so in the man seems, in general; but in the particular it there to always for each man a few animals whose the resemblance dominated in him, and that influence as his character.

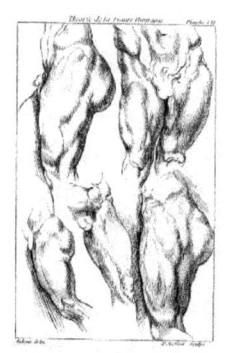

The Plate VII and VIII, offer one confirmation Of this principle in the buttock and the thighs, so that in the arms and the shoulders of the men kind and nervous, whose the muscles appearance have a lot of resemblance with the same parts of the animals aforesaid.

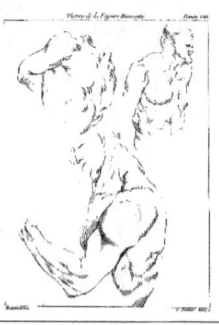

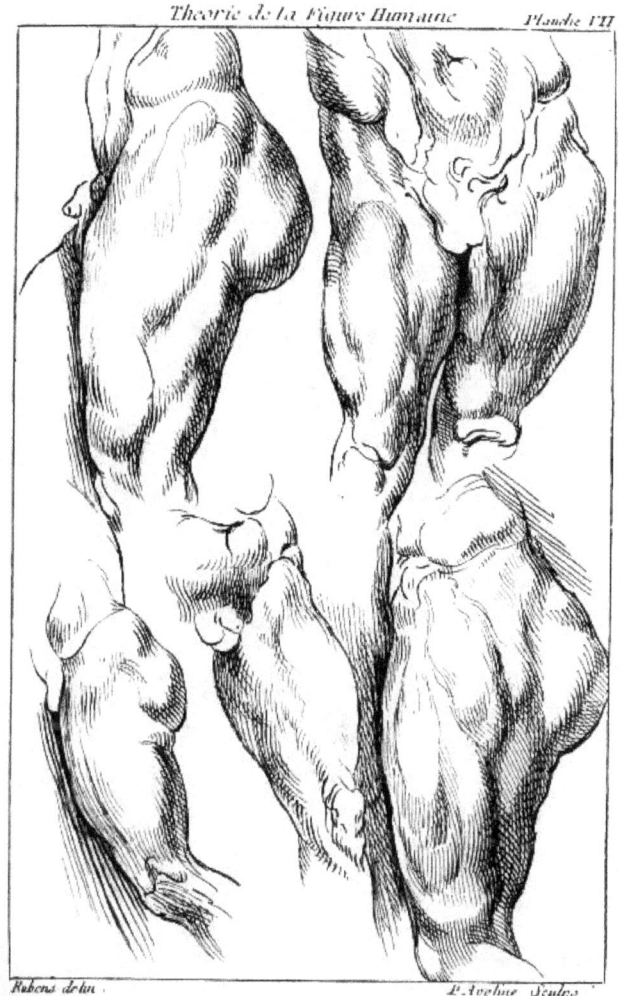

Rubens delin.   P. Aveline Sculps.

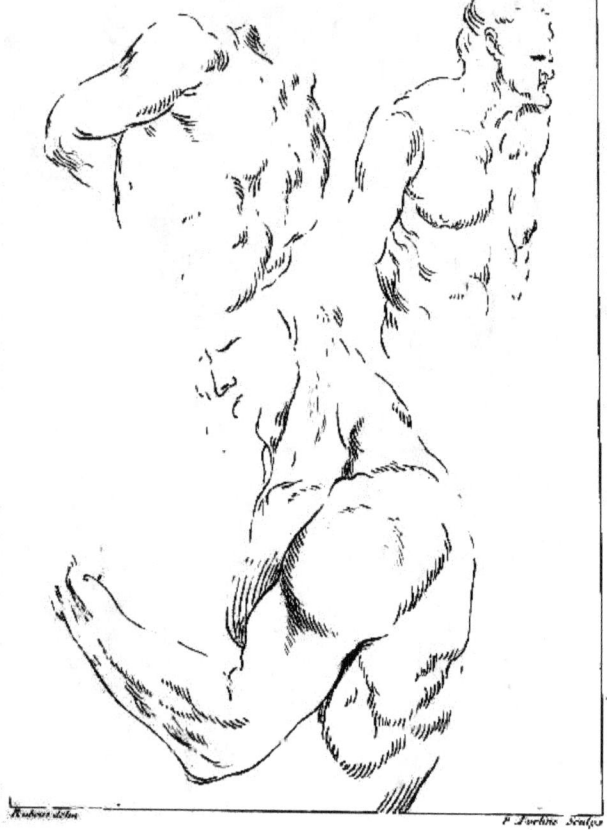

Rubens delin.   *P. Tardieu Sculps.*

Chapter III.
Of the figure human consider in his repose.

One figure is in his repose when the equilibrium as exactly guard, it not himself moves or not himself incline of none side, but it rest constantly in the situation or it himself find: it is the state of the bodies ponderous and robust. We in have a very beautiful example in the statue of the Emperor Convenient, who himself see to Rome in the gardens of Vatican, appeal vulgarly it Belvedere (Gazebo). It there is represent under the clothing and the resemblance of Hercules, hanging rail a child as his arms graceless. We admire above all the attitudes of the figures who appear duty if stop, or of those who appear willing at to leave the rest for himself to put in movement. We find an example worthy of the more grand praises of the first of these attitudes in the statue of Antinoüs (vulgarly the Lantin) that the we see to Rome, in the same garden of Vatican, whose the limbs are willing with so of art that we think that the figure proceed pass of movement the rest, and this with one vivacity and one promptness extraordinaire.

We see an example of second kind in all its beauty and its perfection in the statue of Apollo who is the even place, who seems want exit of the state of rest for himself put in movement. It is good surprising that these two masterpieces inimitable of the more scholarly antiquity have could himself conserve until we wholesome and whole the middle of the wars cruel, of the looting and of the calamity without number who have havoc the Italy since so of age, and that they have resists to the ruined entire and to the destruction of the Empire Roman.

It there a one other attitude mixed who participle of the figure standing and of that who is lying: it is when the part lower of body, since the hip or the top of the thigh until the sole of the feet, is supported as one alone leg, the part higher of bodies himself finding supported as some support. Such are the statue of Hercules that we see in the court of palace Farnese: that of Silenus, feeder of Bacchus, in the garden of Medicis, that of Faune dreamer, the palace Justinian: that of one other Faune play the flute, in the village Borghese, and quantity of others statues that we see to Rome, which himself reply more or less as the support who the maintain.

Baccio Bondinelli to represent of even with as much of art than of intelligence of the man in diverse attitudes, in his tables of massacre of the Innocent, whose we coveted the engraving. The antique we have also leash of the statues in of the attitudes differences of she that we just of describe, but who appear in full movement. Of this number are the figure of Gladiator in the village Boghese, who of one not impetuous himself prepare to carry a coup to his opponent, and parry in actual time that who the menace: or good, in the garden of Medicis, the children of Niobe, who appear want whether escape for themselves purloin to the fury of Apollo and of Diana who the continue to knocking of flitch. Such are again these figure in action that we see in the representation of the battles: that of Alexander taming the horse Bucephale, the mountain Quirinal to Rome, Etc.

Of the different statues ancient.
The Sculptures of the antiquity not
themselves make step withdrawn in the
bounds narrow of the examples previous,
although they have varied to the infinite
the attitudes and the adjustments of their
statues: they have represented the one
standing and in rest, the other seated. We
to an example inimitable of this latest in
the group famous of Laocoon dregs with
his children by of the serpent monstrous
who if kink around of their body, whether
them we see the Belvedere in the garden
of Vatican. This masterpiece of the art is
preferable to all this that the antiquity to
product of more beautiful, is in painting, is
in sculpture; also good that the statue of
the death who himself rests, softened by
them caresses of Cupid, or the Love, in
the garden of Ludovise, to Rome. We see
finally of the figures curvy, as that of the
man who sharpens an iron, in the garden
of Medicis: those of the striver, the even
place. Of the figure lying, as we represent
the Gods-Rivers: of other who appear to
sleep, as that of Cupid, and that of the
Hermaphrodite, in the village Borghese,
beyond of the door called Salaria: of the
figure overwhelmed of languor, as that of
Mirmille dying, in the garden of Ludovise:
that of Cleopatra expiring, the Vatican:

that of Venus languishing, in the village Borghese. We in see children totally in the arms of the death, as that of one of the children of Niobe, in the gardens of Medicis, etc. But in here enough for this who regard the men; speak to present of the statues of females.

This one differs of the men in this what is more fearful and more weak, by that his center of gravity, who past in the node of the throat, not respond not exactly and perpendicularly at center of equilibrium who must himself find the middle of low of the leg, as this himself see in the man standing and in repose: the place that in the female, the line perpendicular lowered of node of his throat, proceed lead to the interior of heel of foot who support the weight of bodies, as we can him see in the statue of Venus happy, called also Venus celestial, and of the Venus incumbent of bath; all the two in the garden of Vatican; and in a lot of others figures of females. In a word, we can remark in the beauty statue of Venus Aphrodite, or the Greek, who is to Rome, in the gardens of Medicis, assembly complete of all the beauties and perfections that we can desire in one female.

Among the grand number of statues different who himself see of all parts in the village and in the area of Rome, in this way that in his gardens, villages, palace, and houses of particulars, we will pass in review those who take the first rank, and that we regard to just title like this as much of models of perfection, to that those who searching to acquainted this that it there at of more beautiful and of more learned in the sculptures and the painting, so for the design and the just proportion of limbs, that for the movements, the attitudes, the differences contour of figures who constituent the beauty of bodies human, can the admire, measure, and search carefully in all their parts, and take of each this be susceptible of imitation. We begin by the statues of men.

The statue of Hercules, at the palace Farnese: that of the Emperor Convenient, under the figure of Hercules, to Belvedere: those of Antonius and of Apollo, at the same location: the famous statute of Laocoon seated, with his chlldren embarrassed in the gnarl of the serpent: that of Gladiator, to the village Borghese, at Rome.

For the statues of females, one alone we suffice: it is that of Venus Aphrodite, at the Palace of Medicis. We believe that the artists will enjoy a lot of the examination reflexive of these statues of the one and the other sex, who make as much of models of the more grand perfection. We himself merely so of the examples that we just of report; because if the we want to himself to expand as the beautiful of all these figures, this would go to the infinite. We deal following after all this who regard the distinction of these different statues devoted by the antiquity, by their grandeur and by the characters which they were dedicated; of as much more than this part regard rather the history than the art of the sculptures.

Of the Ponderation.

Of the inequality of weights in the figure human, spring the movement, so that we the viewer by this figure Ire of the plate IX, who himself find compulsory or of himself move, or of fall. In all the movements, is prompt or delayed, the man to always the part superior of body more drooping of side as which he himself supported: and the shoulder is more lower and more collapsed is fixed, and who serves of support to all the body.

Theorie de la Figure Humaine Planche IX

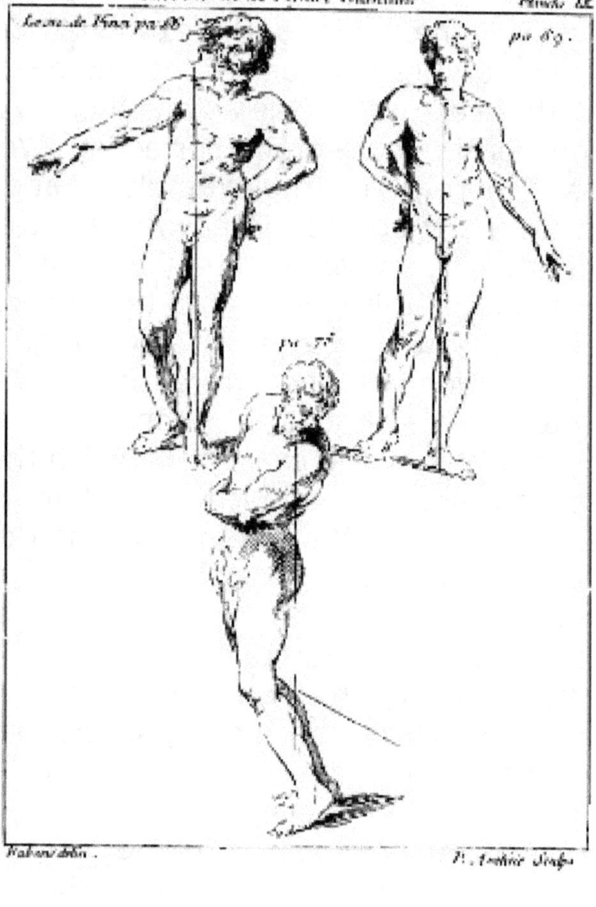

Rubens delin. *P. Aveline Sculp.*

The figure II of the same plate fact see the posture of the men standing without movement, or the shoulder is always more lower of side of the leg as which the figure is posed. Or the repose or the privation of movement comes from of the equality of the weighting as the center. For the locate, he must lower of node of the throat one perpendicular as the middle due low of the leg, or is him center of equilibrium of weight superior, divide evenly: of strength that the center of gravity responds perpendicularly to the center of support.

The figure III represent the manner whose all the limbs of one figure have to be disposes, for that in bending the bodies, the man can revert the head in backside and look at his heels. It is the more grand contortion whose he is capable; and this not himself will point support sentence and support that he writhe the knees and the hunches in direction contrary, and that he not lowered a lot the should of side or the regard in base.

When threshold the arms behind the backside, as the waist (kidney area), the elbows not can never whether approach more near that of the length since the elbow until end of more longer finger of the hand: the arms being so seats, the part superior of bodies, seen by behind, form a square perfect. Plate X, Fig. I. The more grand extension of arms above the stomach is of might make arrive the elbow until middle of bodies. Here in pressing the hand as the shoulder, and the elbow himself locate the middle of the chest, the two shoulders and the two parts of arms bend format a triangle equilateral. Plate X, fig II.

When the man himself willing to strike a stroke with violence, he himself bend and himself diverted as much that he can of side opposite to that or he to design of strike. So he collects all the force whose he is able, for the carry and the discharge then as the thing that he wants attain, by a movement compose. To see the fig. III, same plate.

The plate XI and XII represent the bodies human standing, in divers postures and attitudes, is straight or leaning.

We see as the plate XIII diverse statues ancient, they that of Hercules of palace Farnese, of the Emperor Commode (Convenient) under the figure of Hercules, etc.

The Plates XIV and XV offer different figure in of the attitudes highly-varied, them each standing, the other common, of other to knees, etc.

Leon de   Vinci pa 76   pa.76.

pa.76

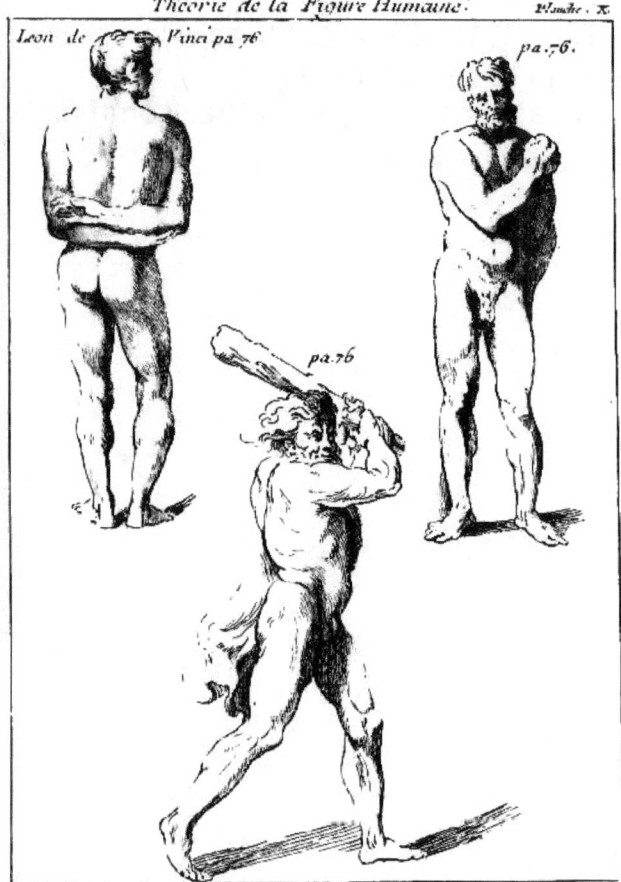

Rubens delin.   P. Aveline Sculps.

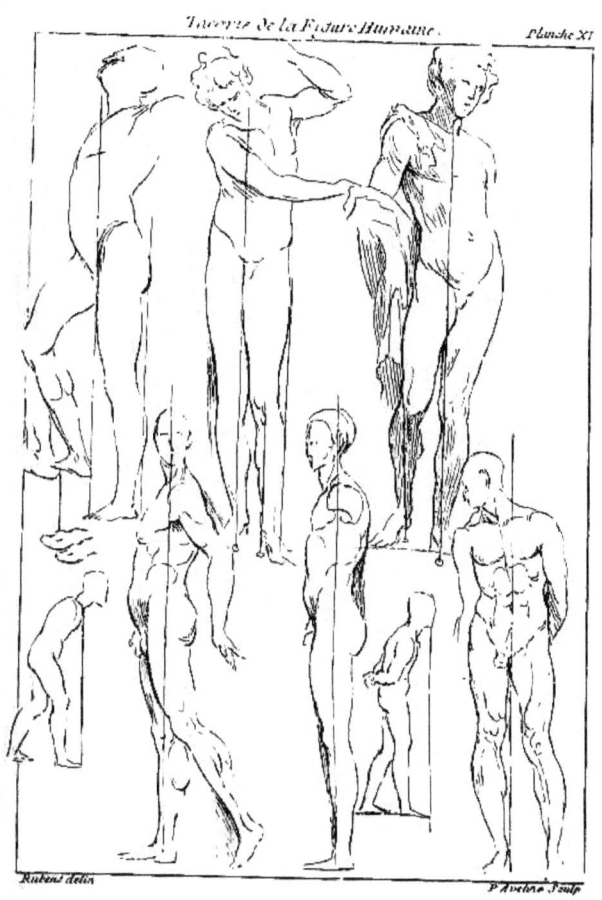

Rubens delin   P. Aveline Sculp

45

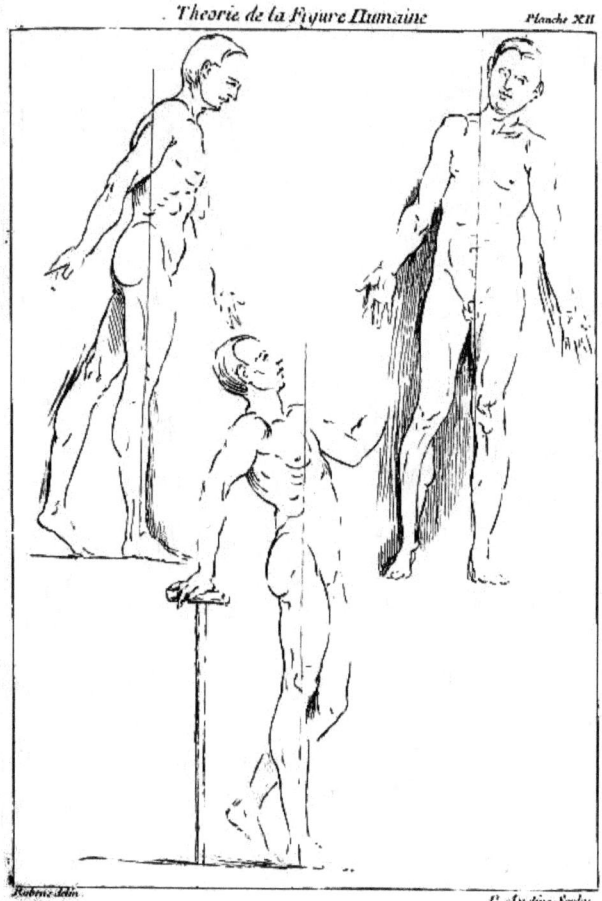

Rubens delin.

P. Aveline Sculps.

46

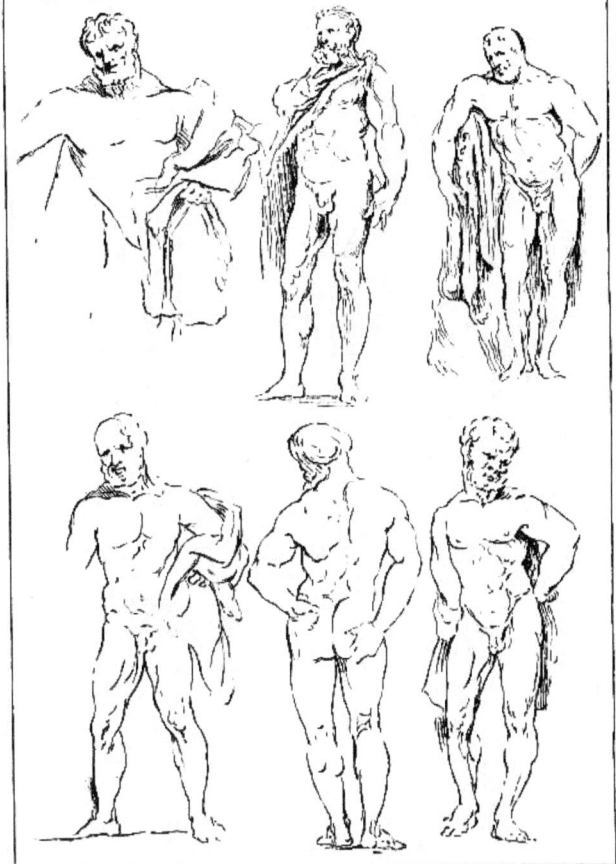

Rubens delin.   P.Aveline Sculps

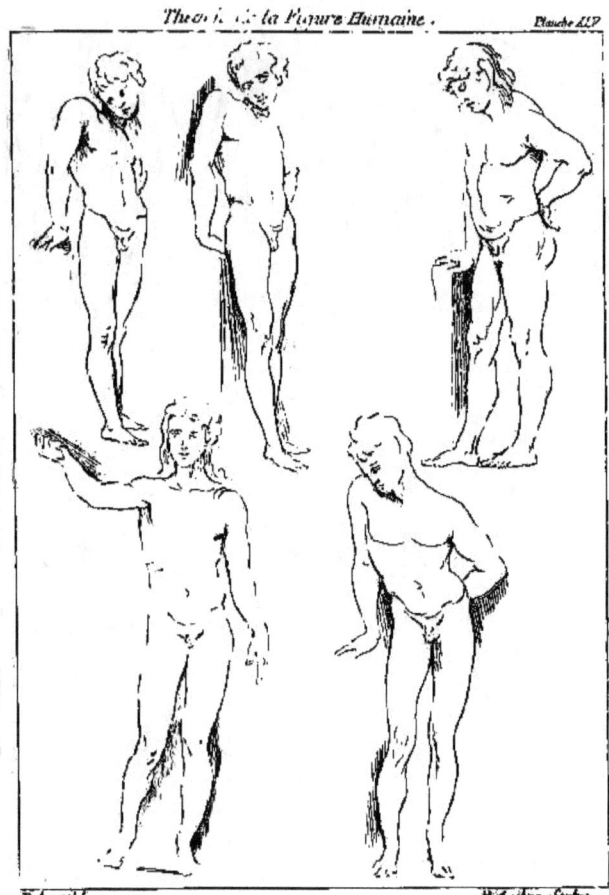

Rubens delin.   H.Aveline Sculps

48

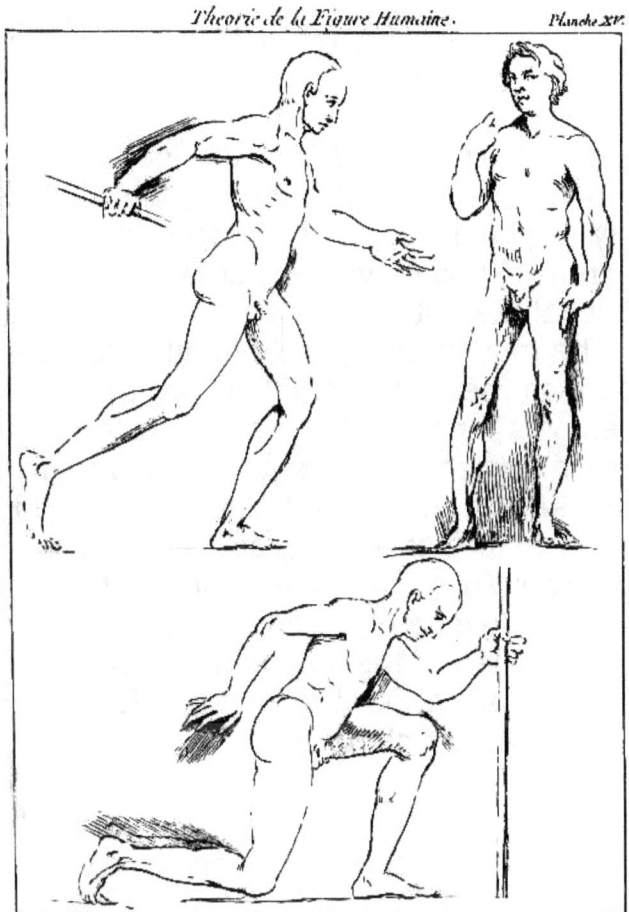

Rubens delin.   *P. Aveline Sculp*

Chapter IV.
Of the figure human consider in his movements.

The movements of human can himself report at five species different; know: the movement natural, the mental, the corporeal, the mixed, and the local.

We call movement natural, him by the way whose a bodies can if increase and decrease: this movement or is of any utility the artist.

The movements purely mental deposes so much the bodies of all action, that it seems as if he strait dead. In effect, as he acts in neglecting absolutely all movement outside, the limb of body languishes, and are in a state of repose; and sort that it not orders no sign of life or of breathing.

The movement purely corporeal not product than of the gestures empty of meaning, such that those of one foolish, or of one man drunk, or in the delirium.

The movement becomes mixed when the corporeal is joint the mental. In this reunion, before things, the looks of the figure himself direct towards the object as which the mind resolved of make to act the body. Then, little by little, the limbs themselves dispose accordance the movement mental, to that acting by of the attitude suitable, they make that the thought offers at execute.

The movement local is that by which a body himself carry of one place in one other. It himself fact or willingly, or with precipitation, or seriously and footstep to footstep, or violently, as removed, or results, or threshold. The artist owes to if apply as all at good acquainted all these movements that we will explain in the examples following.

Application of the principles of movement at of the examples.

One artist finds much from difficult to good voice the pride, the promptness, the vivacity, the agility, the effort, and other things similar, of one athlete full of ardor, and of courage, in which he must make appear of the force, and not step of the stiffness; especially more that all stiffness in the limbs fact always an evil effect, at less that it not whether of one body dead.

The man who himself prepare for strike a stroke violent, or for launch one feature far of him and with force, diverted the part superior of his bodies since the shoulder until belly button, and the secret completely at the object that it menaces or that it at design of strike. The him present just the part lower of his bodies in contrast with the superior, as much that it in is need for power himself reset in his situation naturally, in withdrawing his arms and the parts superior of his body, who in exist violently apart, for produce a movement more loud. We see as the plate XVI two examples of this even movement, who make very difference is in action or in power. The figure marked A is willing for strike with more of violence, by that the part lower of bodies in contrast with the superior, is turn of side of the object of way at power remove the superior with more of speed. This promptness and this speed make that the body spear in acquires one more grand force, and is envoy more far away. The figure B, or the parts lower of bodies is not enough in contrast with the arms who himself prepare to launch some things, is in one posture good less convenient, and not produce that one weak effort: the movement who in results must participate of the weakness of her force driving, which is a lot lesser in this figure than in the previous, by that it arises if slim not with enough of violence. We can compare this movement to that of one arch who, not being that poorly tense, push to less far the feature that it must launch. Because of the rupture violent born the speed of movement: if it not there at point of violence, it not can step there to have of severance, and by consequent point of movement rapid. From where he follows that the figure A act more mightily than the figure B.

He there to one attitude
Who not is step ordinary, it is when the shoulder is drooping of side whose the foot arise support step the weight of bodies: so all the force fore of the equilibrium of the figure himself find in the haunch and in the kidney(waist). *View the figure A of the plate XVII.*

The man is in one attitude doubtful when threshold as the two feet: it is the posture ordinarily of the people languishing of malady, or fatigue by a labor excessive, or good overwhelmed of one old age decrepit. It is also that of the children, who not have point one capacity assured. *To see the figure B, same plate.*

That who march against the effort of one wind violent, not observe of the step the rules weighting for hold his body in balanced, perpendicularly as his center of support: but it himself looks of as much more in before that the wind breath with more of violence. *Same plate, fig. C.*

The man at more of force for pull than for push, by that in pulling, the muscles of the arm it joins again, which have of force that for pull only, and not for push. This just also of muscle A B (pate XVIII, figure of in low) who serves to flex the arm, who is more strong and more elongate of the pole of the elbow, as above of arm, than the muscle D E who is below, who extends the arm, and who is more weak, being more close of center of same elbow C. This movement is product by one force simple who is that of the arm, and also by one force composed, when it the power of the arm we added that of weight of all the bodies, as we it will in the example of the it plate following.

We see as this plate XIX, that these two men act more mightily than in the example precedent, by that it joins right here to the force of the arm him weight of the all him body, and of more the force of the waist, of the legs, and of the hock (back of the knee). Were there see also the difference of that who pull of with that who drawn to him: in this that for pull, besides the weight of bodies, the force of the arms it joint, so than that of the extension of the legs and of the chine (spine), and still that of the muscles of the stomach, more or less, according to that the posture slanting of the man there is necessary: the place that when men pull something, whatever the same parts there concurrent, withal the force of the arm there is without any effect, by that to push with an arm extended all straight and without movement, this not help in nothing advantage than if the we to have a morsel of wood enter the shoulder and the thing that the we pull. The plate XX represents diverse figures nude and dressed, in the attitudes of cover.

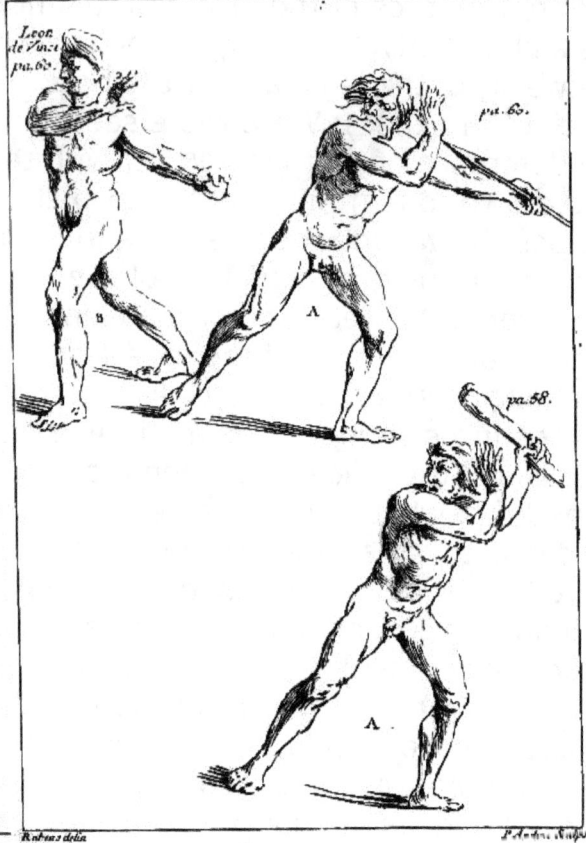

Leon.
de Vinci
pa. 62.

pa. 60.

B

A

pa. 58.

A

Rubens delin.   F. Andre Sculp.

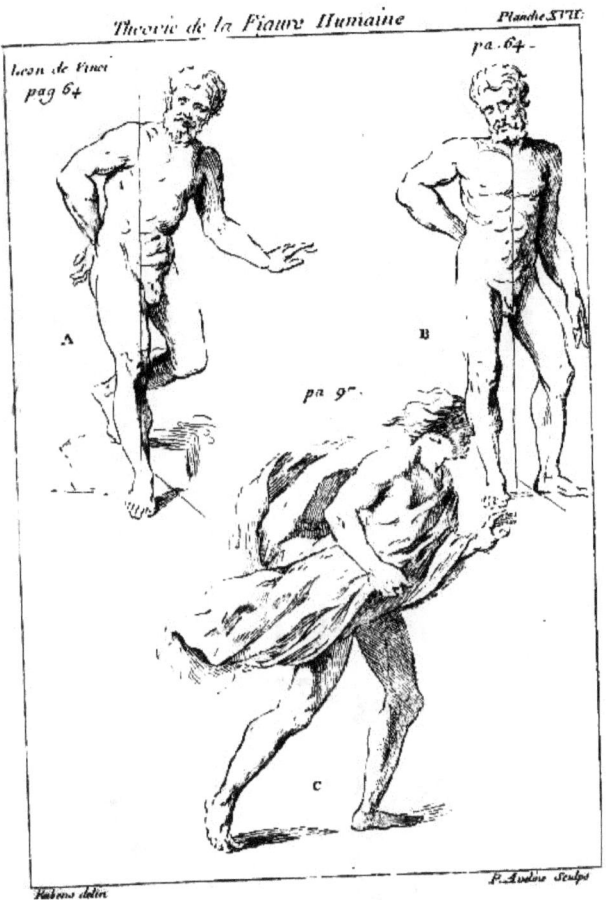

Leon de Vinci
pag 64

pa.64.

pa 9.

A

B

C

Rubens delin   P. Aveline Sculps

57

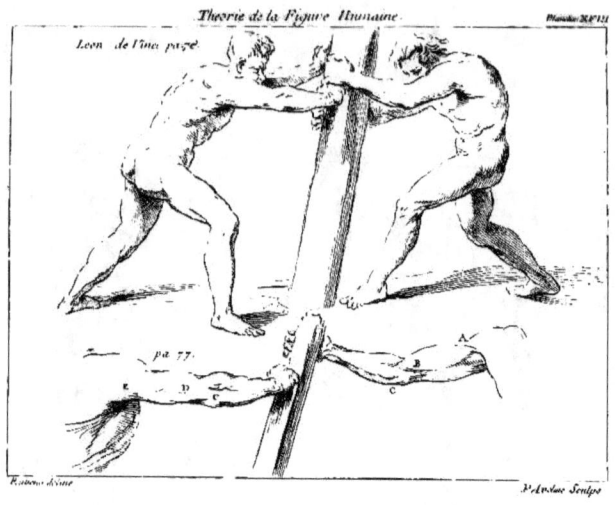

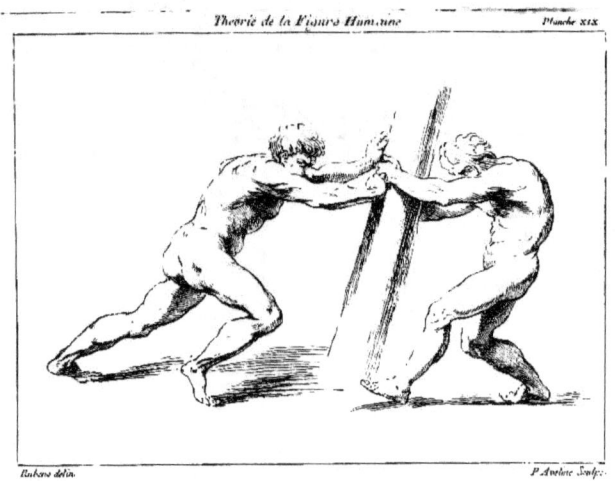

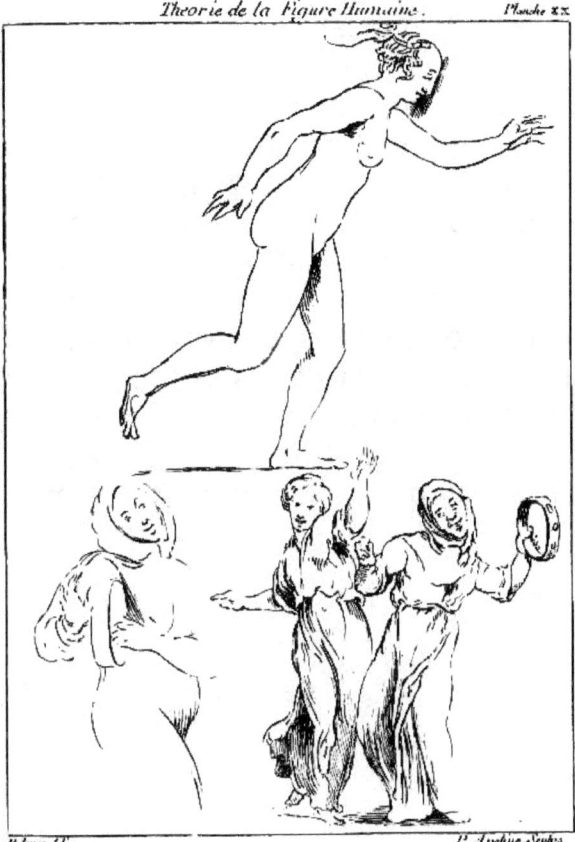

Rubens Delin   P. Avelne Sculps

59

Of the figures who carry thing.
The shoulder as which a man threshold a
burden is always more high than the
other, as if it himself receives rise of if
elevate against the weight who the press.
In all the figures laden, the nature
opposes of a side as much of weight
natural that it himself find of weight
accidental of the other side, of manner
that the center of gravity, is natural or
artificial, must respond perpendicularly as
the center of equilibrium: without what,
the figure not ability himself support,
would fall infallibly. To see the figures 1
and 2 of the plate XXI. It is this that
Leonard of Vinci explain in these terms:

Always the shoulder of the man who threshold a burden is more high than the other shoulder who it is point laden; and this himself see in the figure see in the figure next (plate. 21. fig.2), by which past the line centered of all the gravity of body of the man and of his burden, which mixed and composition of gravity, if this it is that it himself sharing with one equal ponderation as the center of the leg who support the burden, it would necessarily that all if in should go by land. But the nature, in this necessity, provides to make that one such part of the gravity of body of the man, of throws of the other side opposite to this burden extraneous, for him give the equilibrium and the counterweight: and this not himself can make without that the man come to himself bend of side the more lightweight, until this that by this curvature he the make participate to this weight accidental whose he is load. And this again not himself can make if the shoulder who support the burden not himself rise, and that the shoulder feathery and without loading himself lower: and it is the expedient whose the industrious necessity himself serves in one such get together. Leonard of Vinci, Chapter. CC.

The figure I ^{re} of the same plate fact see that the man who walking, loading or not, must to have the center of his gravity as the center of the leg who pose to land.

The weighting, or the equilibrium of the figure the figure human, himself divided in two parties; know the simple and the compound: the equilibrium simple is that than the man fact resident standing as his feet without himself move, By the equilibrium composed, we hear that than fact a man when at as him some burden, and that it the support by of the movement various, as in the figure 3 of this same plate, representing Hercules who muffled Anthée, which having raises from land, and the shaking with his arms against the chest, he must that it himself given in counterweight as much of charge of his own limbs behind the line central of his two feet, as the center of the gravity huge of Anthee is in ahead of the same line central of the feet. *Leonard of Vinci, Chapter CCLXIII.*

Of the Athletes.

The gait of the Athletes to something of more proud and of more sublime than that of the other men. Virgil in to fact of the painting worthy of admiration in the fifth book of the Aeneid. To see the figures of Dares and of Entellus, marked A and B, as the plate XXII.

> Such a first Dares head high in battles taketh,
> Show shoulders widespread, alternate greedy
> Arms stretching, and vibrant stroke air.

It is so that Dares amounting her head arrogant, if advanced proudly in the arena, and himself present it first the combat. The discover his wide shoulder, the extends his arms nervous, and the waving alternately, the beating the air to knocking reduplicate.

> This start, double from shoulders throws apparel:
> And great joint fitted, great bones, muscular
> extract, equally great media consists arena.

To these words Entellus having throws low the clothing who him covering the shoulders, fact see the strong joints of his limbs, his grand bones, and his arm vigorous: the walking boldly, and seem as a giant the middle of the arena.

> Confirm in fingers forthwith erect both,
> Forearms to surpass fearless lifted air.

Raising back long heads difficult from stroke,
Spar with his hands, fight assail.

Immediately the two Athletes himself stand as the point of the feet, and of one air intrepid they elevate the arms in the air for himself hit: each withdrawn neatly his head in back for the steal the knocking furious of his opponent. They if approaching, they himself join, and himself seizing the one the other by the hands, the fight begins.

I have said, stood on the opposite side of the mouths of the young bull, He stood gift battle; harsh and reduced poised right hand midway between the horns girth arduous, ratified and dashed into the bones of the brain.
Struck down as an ox fallen down dead on the ground, which falls to his knees trembling.
Virgil. Aeneid. book. V.

He says, and if advancing towards the bull who was the price of his victory, he Survey his arms formidable armed of gesture, he leaps, and swaying his stroke, it the striking with force enter the two horns: the skull shatter sinks in the brain: the animal trembles, totter, and falls dead as the place. Aeneid. Book. V.

Daniel of Volterre at very good represents the Wrestlers; in the first place, when himself threaten, when if approaching, when in come the hands, and to see the two figures marked A, and the group B, as the plate XXIII.

The Athletes himself stand the combat the bodies naked, the skin oily, rubbed and disgusting of oil. It is thus, the report of Vitruvian, that the architect Dinocrate himself presented in front of Alexandre: he was naked, at the manner of the Athletes, the bodies gleaming of oil, having as the head one crowned of poplar, wearing as the shoulder left the bare of a lion, and talking of the hand right one strong mace bristly of knots. Vitruvian, Preface of Book II.

There is to have one law in the Spartans who their defended of himself deliver to one certain softness, or of acquire an overweight capable of harm the square-bashing that they were obliges of make.

We see as the plate XXIV Laocoon who if sought of himself get rid of owing snake who the surrounds: Hercules upright a boar of one greatness huge; and the same easing Atlas of weight immense of the atmosphere. Ovid in spoken in these terms, (Book. II. of his metamorphoses

Atlas in himself laborite,
Hardly what their shoulders splendor supports axis.

Ovid. expelling. book. 2.

See Atlas himself ready to succumb under the weight huge of world celestial that he threshold as his shoulders.

Bulk under immense after desiccator Atlas,
Betrayed Hercules strength this near you toil.

When Atlas, fatigue of weight immense of the atmosphere, began to dwindle, this labor too much annoying for him was entrusted the strengths invincible of vigorous Hercules.

The plate XXV represent a few figures effect and in the repose.

We see as the plate XXVI and XXVII, plate figure of men layers by land, death, or expiring; such that Dares, defeated and terrace by Entellus; Virgile the represent so to half death.

Boasting both sides head, thick and blood,
Mouth rejecting thing, gore at bloody teeth.

Virgil. Aeneld. book. V.

He waves, he said, his head of side and of other, vomiting a blood thick: the teeth out of the mouth melee with of the waves of blood.

To the end of combat of Enée (Aeneas) against Turnus (Hercules), the finish so his admirable pome

> This saying, (iron) point of an arrow against under pectoris (breast) conduit enthusiastically. Asturum they prolapse cold limbs, Life with sigh flees displeasure under shadows.
>
> Virgil. Aeneid. lib. XII

At these words, Enée, transport of anger, him broken his sword in the middle of the chest. So a cold mortal if seized of Turnus, and him ice the blood in the veins, his limbs himself stiffening, he makes the last sigh, and his soul indignant escapes into the air in shoving of longs wailing. *Virgile, ibid.*

The plates XXXVIII and XXIX represents of the men crucifies, and contribute, with the two plates previous, for demonstrate that the line right is the element of the bodies dead: and it is the alone case or he is suitable of make appear of the stiffness in the limbs, as we the at already observe heretofore.

We see as the plates XXX and XXXI diverse attitudes of angles flying, and of figures abducted as of the clouds.

The plate XXXII offer one composition of Rubens, inmates of a low relief antique or the is see Satyr castigates by another Satyr in the honor of God of the Gardens.

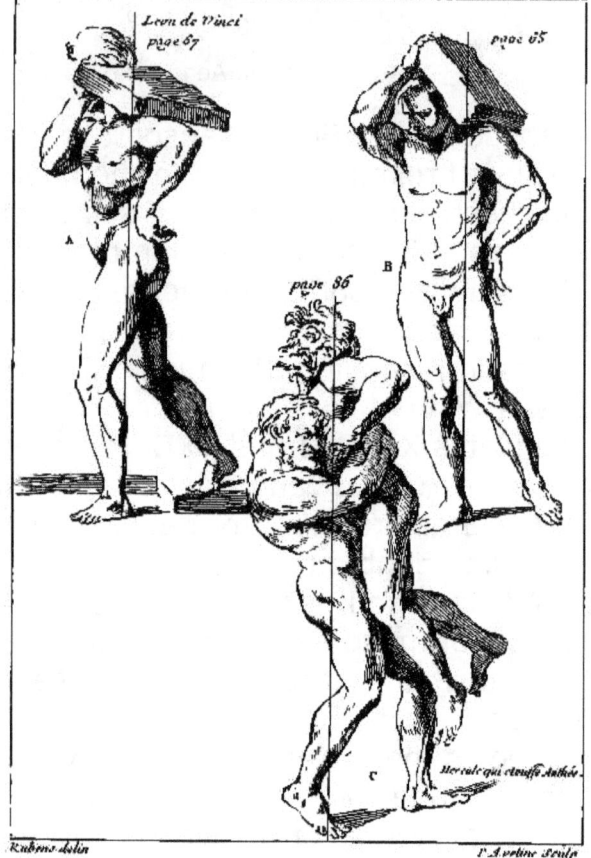

Leon de Vinci
page 67

page 65

page 86

A

B

C

Hercule qui etouffe Anthée

Rubens delin

l'Avoline Sculp

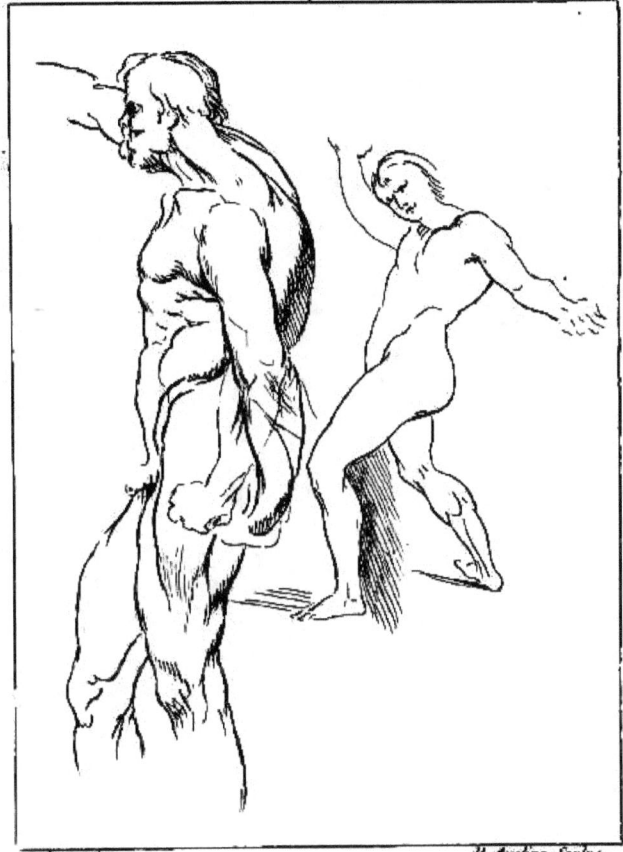

Rubens delin.   P. Aveline Sculps.

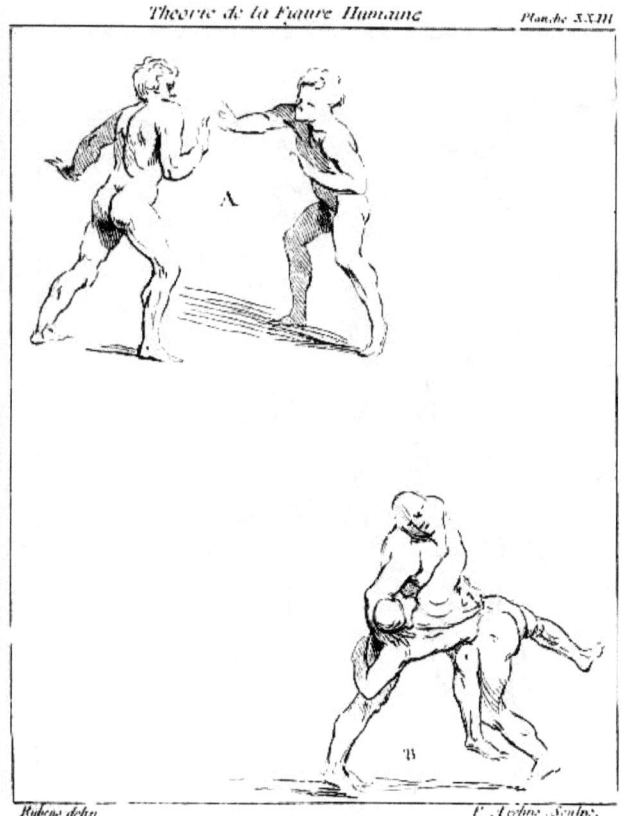

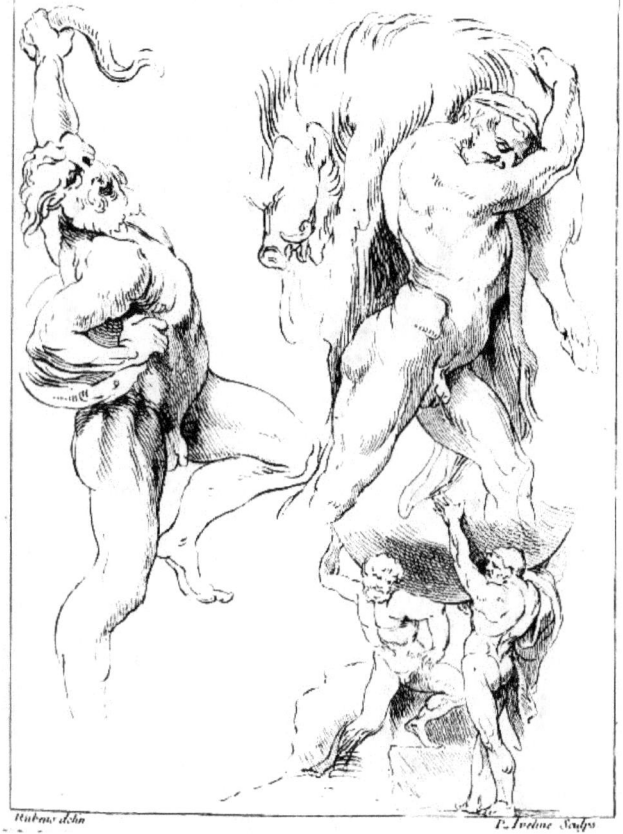

Rubens delin   P. Tvelnc Sculps

71

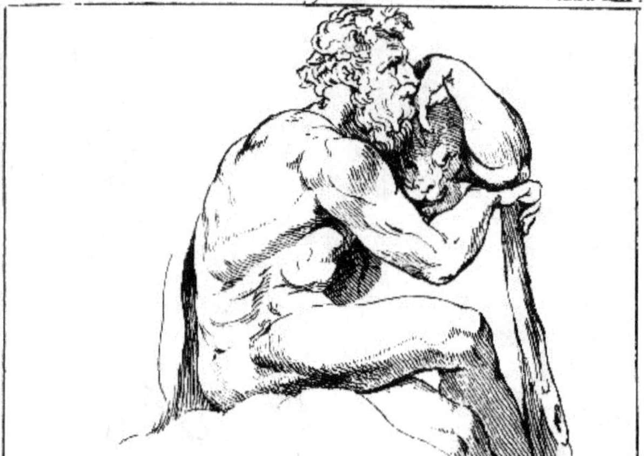

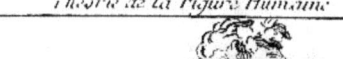

Rubens delin.   P.Aveline Sculps.

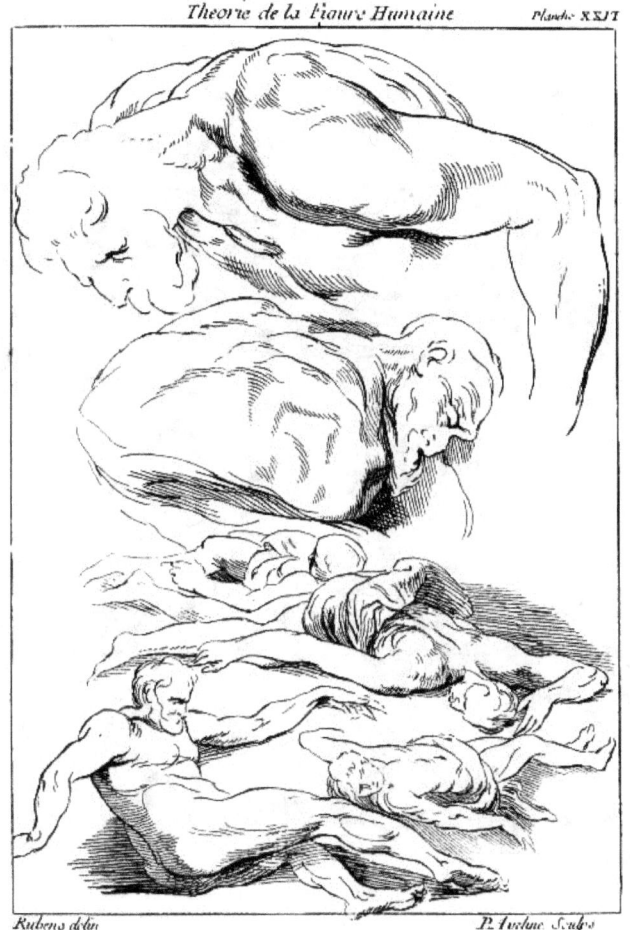

Rubens delin   P. Avelne Sculps

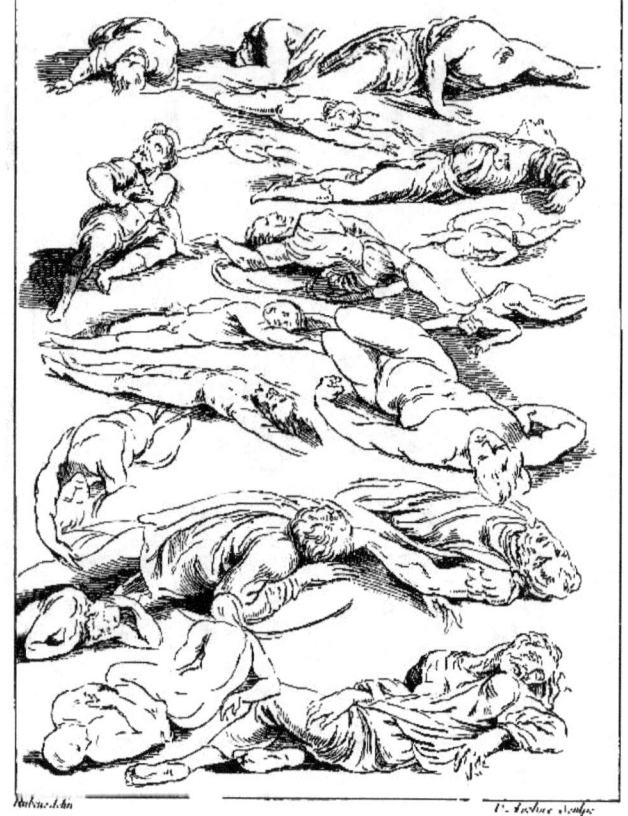

Rubens delin.   P. Aveline Sculp.

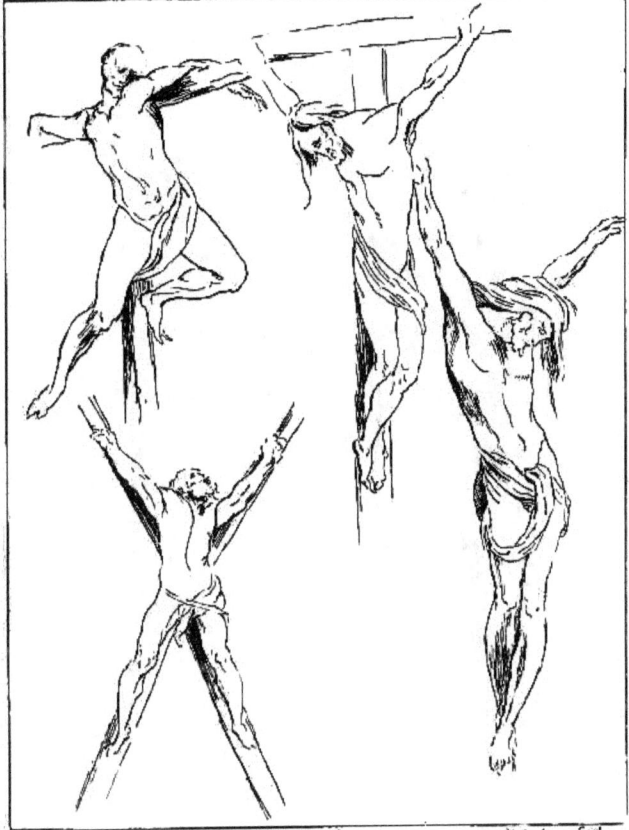

Babonsddin   l'Aveline Sculps

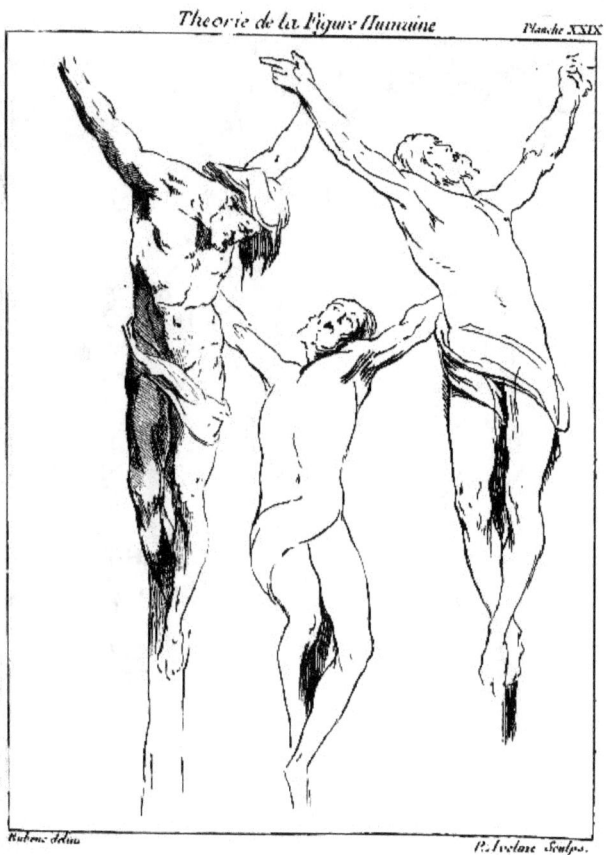

Rubens delin.   P. Avelane Sculps.

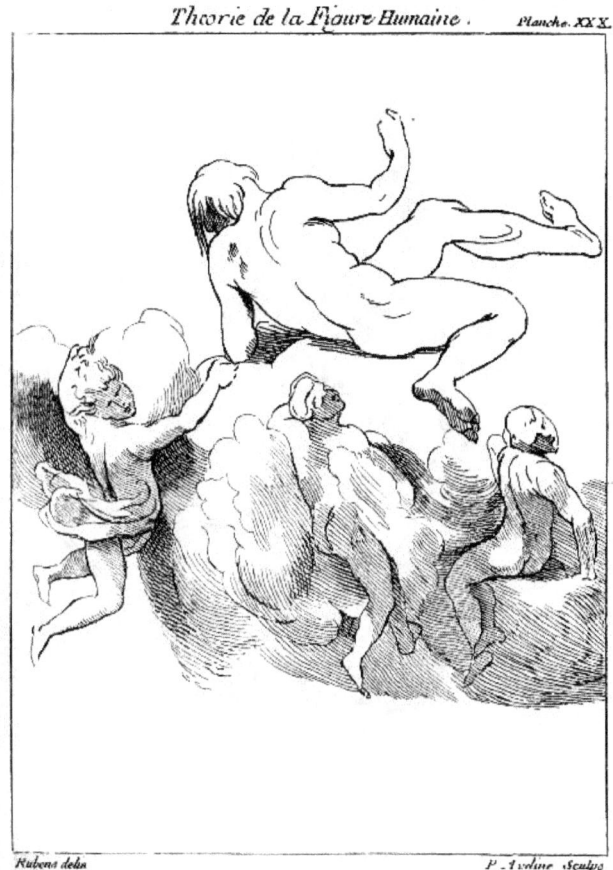

Rubens delin   P. Aveline Sculps

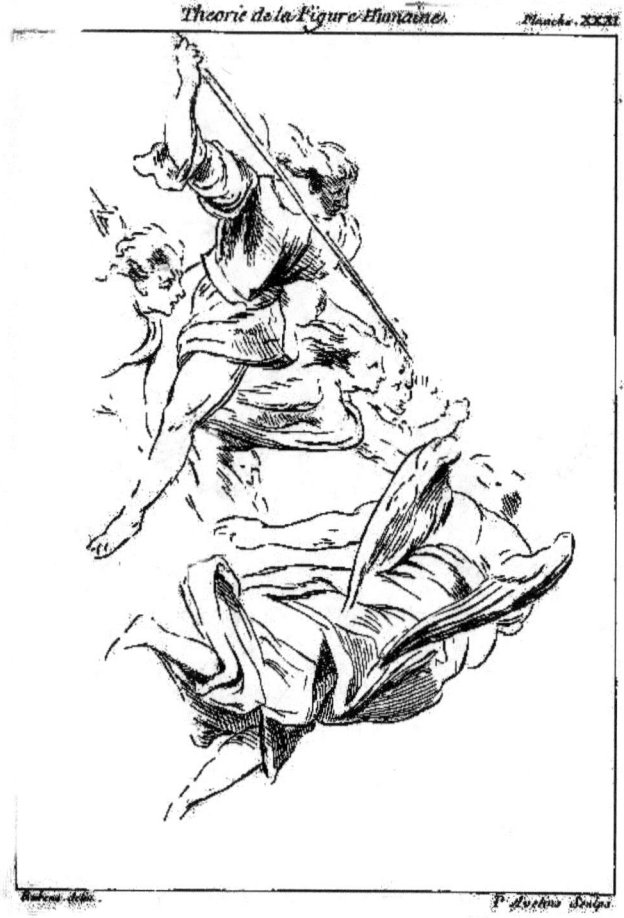

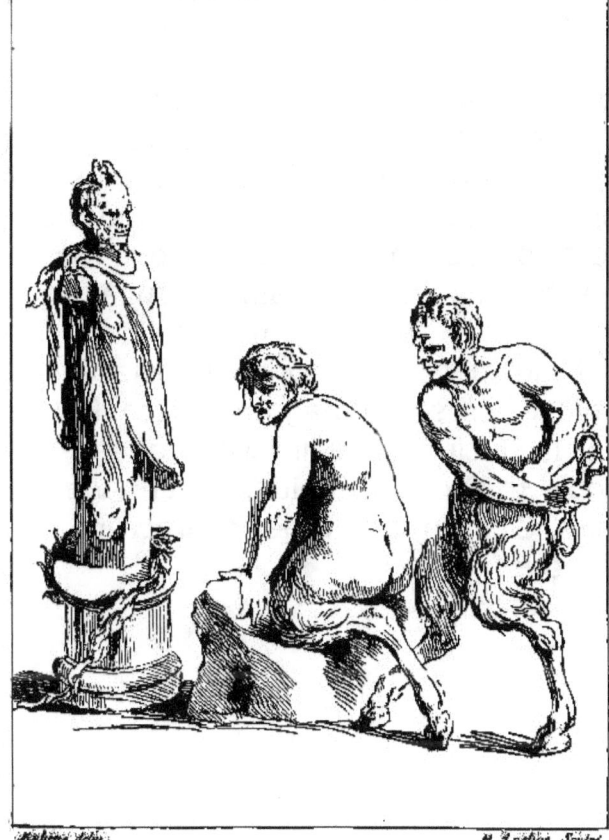

Rubens delin.   P. Aveline Sculps.

Chapter V (5)

Of the different species of statue of the ancient.

We distinguish seven species of statues; known, the similar, the grand, the more grand, the very grand, the small, the more small, and the very small.

We call statues similar, when the characters that they represent are in their proportions naturel. We elevated these the people of one merit distinguish, and the wise or philosophers of reputation. We might for example, in train of similar to Armodius (Competent), Aristogeiton (Aristotle), Homer, Solon, Hippocrates, Gorgias, Berose, Pythagoras, Plato, Brutus, Quintus Mucius, to Clelie, wife robust, the Catons, to Quintus Ennius, Marcus Varron, Virgile, Ciceron, and other characters illustrious.

The statues are said grand when overage of half the proportion ordinarily: they them has called Augusta, by that in elevated of similar the Kings and Emperors, as to Phoroneus (Taxes), Lycurgus, Themistocles, Xerces (Fallow), Alexander, Romulus, Numa (Synonyms), Tatius (Tati), Cneius Pompey (Kneios Pompeo), Cesar, August, and the other Emperors Romans who have prime pupil the rank of the Gods. It is in this idea, to this that I thought, that the Queen Dido, ready to render the last sighing, exclaims: "My image perishes so with me in the tomb"

And now I great mine under earth shall go image!

It seems himself complain over there of this that refuse of him erect one statue, and of make his apotheosis after his death, by that it was the usage among the ancients of not point accord this honor to those who were to given voluntary the death.

The statues more grand were of one proportion double of the grandeur ordinarily: we in erected only the heroes, as to Bacchus Hercules, Theseus, and to of other similar.

The statues very grand are of triple of the grandeur ordinary of the figure human. We there to given the names of *colossus,* is by they are hollow inside, is that this named derived from two words Greek μάγγος, magnus, and ωκύλος. oculus, as if is distort grand to the view: of other different than these statues have been so called of name of a certain *Colossus*, their inventor. What that it in is, these colossuses arise suitable that only Gods the more powerful, such that Jupiter, (Minerve Greek goddess), Apollo, Mars, and the others Divinities similar; it is so wrong to propose that of the Emperors Romans, and a few Kings among the nations barbarians, have alleged to this honor, so has that of the arc of triumph, the report of Pline, who assures than the Emperor Nero to have ordered that the painted as of the canvas, in one proportion colossus of cxx feet of height. Pline, book. XXV, chapter. VII. He says also that Phidias to have fact two figures in mantle, that Catulus (Young) placed in the temple of the Fortune to Rome, with one other figure colossal who strait nude. Pline, book. XXXV, chapter. VIII. There is to have at Rhodes one statue colossal of Sun, done in brass by Charles, elevated of Lyfippe, who to have LXX cubits of high. It was situated at the entry of harbor of Rhodes, and the ships pass a full sails enter his leg. It to summer regarded to just heading as one of the seven marvels of world. We in speak following after more the long.

We call small statues those who make below of the greatness human: here is Their proportions. Dividing the height ordinary of the man in four parts equals, We given three of these parts to the statue, who himself find so of a quarter more small than those that nominated similar.

The statues make say more small them when height is reduce to the half of the grandeur ordinary of the figure human. Those that call very small, have that the quarter of this same height.

Here is, this myself seem, the reason of this diversity of grandeur in the statues. The shortage of metal. Or the ease of transport to occasion the small: the magnificence, or the dignity of character that want to represent, in to fact elevate a few ones until the height of hundred cubits and further. Is it not just in effect than those who have dominated as the other while them life by them courage, of by the dignity of them employment, the important also after them death as the common of the men by the grandeur and the excellence of the monument that them high? It is that Homer wants make hear by the towards following, when we represent the Goddess Pallas adorning Ulysses of a rich clothing.

Straining multiple from his shoulders Tritonia pallas Composer increased body trailing young (1)

The Goddess Pallas he putting as the shoulders a cloak to grands folds, increases the majesty of his body, and seems the rejuvenate; and he added little after: as if appeared himself admitted already the number of the Gods.

(1) These towards make from of one translation of the two first books of the Iliad in towards Latin, done by *Chamberlain*, *in fourth*, imparts to Strasbourg in 1538.

Virgil to find one expression also happy in the painting that we fact of the astonishment of Dido, Queen of Carthage, to the aspect of Enée (Aeneas) outgoing of the thick cloud whose it to have summer envelope by its mother Venus, who to have had care of beautify her charms, for the make like of Dido.

Resisted Aeneas, sunbeam in cloud shone, prow shoulder and lastly God similar: for indeed herself decorum Cassaria move loosely mother, light and youth Purple, and atone eyes breathed honors.

Aeneas stood still, and appeared in front of the Queen with the more grand shine, the middle of the thick cloud bright whose he was surrounds. He to have the port and the majesty of one God; because the Goddess her mother to have taken if we of beautify her long hair, and she to have widespread one beauty lovely and the grace of the youth in his eyes and in all the features of his face. *Aeneid. Book. I.*

Xenophon reports that Cyrus, after the celebrated Victoria that it slates as the Assyrians, was very attentive at all this who can to contribute at the beauty and at the majesty of his body. And we read in Quint- Curtius than Thalestris, Queen of the Amazons, designed of contempt for

Alexandre the Macedonian when she lives the smallness of her size, and then this was the reason who determined this vanquisher of the Asia to himself make erect, in the place or he to have encamped, one statue more grand than natural: being convinced than this statue of grandeur extraordinaire excite further the admiration of the posterity.

I thought also than it is in the same intention than is to erected at our Emperors of the statues more grands than the natural. And this born just not so (as the thought the vulgar) of this than if we the had made of the proportion ordinary, they would publish too much small, being placed as a monument high, that by than this grandeur as natural their given more of dignity and of majesty.

The statues that is dedicated the Gods, is of greatness ordinary, is more grand, have summer called by the Latins, Image, Idols: such are those of Mars, of Venus, of Minerve, of Cupid, of the Sincerity, of the Fortune, and of the other Divinities who have point the form ordinary of our bodies. The statues for the hero or the half-god, have summer called figurehead

$\xi \acute{o} \alpha \nu \varkappa \varsigma$ (ξόανψς), that is to say, made with scissors, or in removing of the material, as we work the figures in marble, in stone, in wood, Etc. This name to summer given of on board to all the statues in general, mostly at those of the Divinities Egyptians.

(reading note: these are the original old Greek spelling of words that one letter I am not familiar with for make true translation of them from French wording of the book as listed under each reading of passages.)

The statues of the Kings were called andriant ανδραντας, statue: those of the wise, εςκελγς, elect, similes: those that erects it to people of merit, or who had made some service essential at the

ανδριαντας Republic, βροτγς, Vrotsos,
εικελυς humane.
βροτυς

We gave the name of εικονιχης (eikonikis) figurative, to similarity express, the figures whose the features of visage were resemblance, that to say in sculpture, that to say in painting: The Latin they have called due name general images, resemblances.

εικονιχης

In vain dear-heart-is of the names particular for the other statues; to less that not wants the call all *effigies,* representations. Because the word figure not appropriate at outline of a man, of a horse, or of all other things, traced as one surface plane.

Of time of Homer, the Greeks called αγαλματα statues, simulacra, all the trappings who were exposes in the temples the eyes of the spectators; and they in have of as much better retained the name, that by the suite, almost all the trappings of these locations dedicated the Gods not consistory hardly than in of the statues.

All the statues whose the greatness strait above of that of one man ordinary, is appellant in general *signs,* statues: who were more small, *seals*, small statues. It there to have also of other figures who not representative point the body human in full, than the quondam appellant *Hermes, or Stemmata (pedigrees)*, bust of Mercury, or imagery of the ancestors. These bust were doors as of the trunks squares, the each more long, the other more short, whose the mostly alloy in decreasing, in form of sheaths by the low; the modern them have given the name of Terms: we proxy in change the head to will.

It there to have one grand quantity of these bust who represented for the ordinary on head of Mercury, from where they have drawn their name: Hermes, in Greek ερμης, wanting say Mercury. We mediate many of these figures around of the tombs, for conserve the memory of those who there were contained. We to have custom of place the statues of the ancestors, in Latin *pedigrees*, in the vestibules, or in the hall who were to the entry of the houses; what were the brands of nobility and of seniority of the house, before the invention of the arms: consistory in of simple bust, whose we not saw that the head, and whose the collar petty cut the high of the shoulders and of the chest.

Various extracts of the history natural of Pline, on the statues of ancients.

The bronze cask employee commonly the statues of the Gods.
The first than I find to have summer done at Rome of this metal, is that of Ceres: the fresh in were taken as the goods of Spurius Cassius, who, aspirant to the royalty, was slew by his Father.
Of the Gods, the bronze passed the statues of the men, and to of the representations various.

The quondam them gave one color with of bitumen, from where he is of as much more surprising that afterwards we himself is enjoyed to the gild. I not know if this invention is Roman, but it is not ancient among Us. We not rear of the statues that to those whose a few stock deserved the immortality. This was of first for the victories in the games coronations, and as all the games Olympic, or this was the custom to elevate one statue the winners. For those who had defeated three times to these same games, them statues were true to life in the differences parts of bodies, it is why we the name εικονικας figurative, similes resemblance. I not know if this not are not the Athenians who the first have elevated of the statues, by authority public, the 1*

Tyrannicides Harmodios and Aristogeiton; this arrived the same year than the Kings knew hunting of Rome. By one commendable emulation, this usage was then worldwide adopted: since then the places public of the villages municipal were decorated of statues:

and by of the inscriptions as them based, we perpetuated the memory and the dignities of the grands men; in kind than the tombs not were more the only monuments of their memory. Soon the house of the particulars and the galleries became of the places public. This how so that the respect of the client for them patrons imagine of the honorary. *Book XXXIV*, Chapter. *IV, section IX.*

The statues so dedicated were formerly dressed of the toga: we himself rather also to at make of the figures nude, tenant one spade: they representative the youth people who oneself practicing in the gymnasium, and himself nominally Achilles tendon.

The usage Greek is of not is of not nothingness veil, the Roman is the contrary of append one armor as the chest of the statues of the militaries. Caesar, being Dictator, subscribed that in the place who door his name we him in elevate one cuirass; because those who are covered the manner of the Lupercalia are also new that those who have published since little dressed of one coat.

Men naked himself fit represent in the same state or he himself find when was book the Humans: he was naked, the hands linked behind the back. Our writers have remark that the poet L. Accius fit placer in the temple of the Muses her statute of one cut loud great though was loud small. As for the statues equestrian, if recommendable in the Romans, their origin just certainly of the Greeks; but the Greeks began by those at an alone horse, for the winners in the games coronations: those who had defeated to two, or to four horses, in consecrated then the same number: from where is came in we the use of adding even a chariot the statues of the victors. That of the chariot to fix horses, or harnessed of elephants, is came more tardy, and not appeared that under August. Chapter. V section. X.

The usage of represent was a chariot to two horses those who, after their priest, had fact the tower of circus, is not no more fort ancient: that of the statues asked as of the columns ballast further. We in have an example in that of C. (Moenius) Moebius, winner of the quondam Latin, which, following the treaty the people Roman gave the third part of booty of the defeated.

This was him who in his Consulate, year of Rome 416, suspended to the tribune the harangues the prows of the ships taken the Antiates he had defeated. Caïus Duilius received the first the honors of triumph naval for her victory as the fleet of the Carthaginian: her statue is again today in the grand square. We there sees also that of P. Minucius, intendant of the rations. It him was elevate except the threshold Trigeminienne, and the spent in was taking as one contribution that fit the people. I do not know if this was the first honor of this species allowed by the people: the Senate sees awarded previously. Beautiful tradition, if she would have not commenced for of the subjects frivolous! Because we to have elevate to Attus Navius, in front of the Senate, one statue whose the base was burned in the fire who the consume the funeral Publius Clodius. We in erected one, by decree public, to Hermodore, Ephesians, in the square of the Elections, by it interpreted the laws written by the Decemvirs (consular imperium in Latin). We erected one staute to M. Horatius Coclès, for one other reason, and better founded: the to have alone regrowth the enemy as the bridge Sublicien; the statue subsists again. I not flee point surprised no more than the

Sybille has had of the statues near of the tribune the harangues, though there in has three: one that Sixth Pacuvius Taurus, town councilor people, fit elevate, and two who it be by M. Meffala. I should think that these and that of Attus Navius, asked of time of Tarquin the old, be the first, if in the Capitol there in to have not of the Kings who have preceded Chapter V, section XI.

Enter these latest, the statue of Romulus is fans tunic, as that of Camille, in the square the harangues. That of Q. Marcius Tremulus, in front of the temple of Castor (Beaver) and Pollux, was equestrian, also fans tunic, and decrepit of the toga: he to have defeated two time the Samnites, and, by the taking of Anagnia, he to have issued the Romans of tribute.

The statues that must to put the rank of the more ancient, make those that sees in the square the harangues of T. Clelius, L. Rofcius, Sp.Nautius, and C. Fulcinius, you are by the Fidenates in one embassy. The Republic awarded ordinarily this honor to those who, against the law of the people, had summer you are.

It the accord the two brothers P. Junius and T. Coruncanus, who were you are by order of Teuca, Reine of the Illyrian.

He not must forget that, according to our annals, their statues in the square public were of three feet of high: it was so the measure honorable. I forget not no more Cn. Octavius, (or C. Popilius, according to of others), to cause of his word famous the King Antiochus. The Prince promising of him reply, this one, with one baguette it subtlety by hazard, drew a circle around of King, and the forced of him give her reply before it in fortuitous. Having summer kill in this embassy, the Senate him erected one statue in the place the more apparent of the square the harangues. The history said also that awarded one statue to the vestal Taracia Caïa, or Suffetia, for be placed or she would wish: circumstance who is not less honorable for she, that having summer, whatever wife, honored of one statue. Here is, in the own terms of the annals, this who it him merited: "for to have fact prefect the people of field of "Tiber". Pline, Chapter. VI.

I find that lifted of the statue to Pythagoras and to Alcibiades, the two angles of the square of the Elections, when, in the war against the Samnites, the Oracle of Apollo Pythian had ordered of devote in the place the more honorable of the statues the more brave and the more wise of the Greeks.

They subsisted until this that the Dictator Sylla fit build the Senate in this in law. I am surprised of this that the Senators of so have given the preference for the wisdom to Pythagoras as Socrates, who, by the Oracle of same God, to have summer declare the more wise of the men; and that for the value they have the accord to Alcibiades, the prejudice of so of others particularly to that of Themistocles, in who the value and the wisdom were united. We that being so the statues as of the columns, for the elevate the above of the other men. It is also this than signify the new invention of the arc of triumph. However this honor commence in the Greeks: and I think that no one was not as much of statues elevates in his honor than Demetrius of Medallions to Athens, because him in erected three hundred sixty: the year not occasionally not again this number of days. They were almost immediately briefed. The Tribes Roman in had high in all the streets of Rome to C. Marius Gratidianus, they overthrew when Sylla enter in the villa. *Pline, Chapter VI, section XII.*

The statues walking were without doubt very good hour estimated to Rome; however the origin of the statues equestrian is also loud ancient:

we in to same accord the honor to of the women, because there in to one of Clélie, as if this was not pitch enough of to see her decorated of the toga: while that Lucrece and Brutus, who had hunt the Kings for which Clélie was in confinement, not in had point. I should think that this statue and that of Horatius (Horace) Coclès, have summer the first high by decree public, and Pifon (Piso) not upright than this were those who had summer in confinement with Clelie, and that Porfenna (Porsenna) returned to her consideration, who the him erected. Because for that of Attus and those the Sybille, this was Tarquin: for those of the Kings, the is similar they self the erected themselves. The Hérault Annius said the contrary that the statue equestrian who narrow vis-a-vis the temple of Jupiter Stateur (Stator) in the vestibule of palace of Tarquin the Superbe, narrow that of Valeria, girl of Consul Publicola, and what is silent saved alone in passing the Tibre (Tiber) to the swim, the other hostages sent to Porfenna (Porfana) having summer massacred by the parts of the Tarquins in one ambush. Chapter, VI, section. XIII.

Of the way whose the ancient represent their Deities.

The god Mars was honor by the Romans under the two names of Gradivus (Mars) and of Quirinus (Remus): under the first, he to have her stature in the field of Mars, except of the villa: under the second name, her statute narrow placed the middle of *Forum*, in the interior of the village.

Venus was represented, in the Lacédémoniens (Spartans), the arms to the hand. In Arcadie (Arcadia), she was black. In Chypre (Cyprus), she to have of the beard, the scepter virile, of the clothing of women.

In Egypt, the Amour (Love) was represented with of the wings, behind the statue of the Fortune, who was front she one horn of abundance.

In the Thessalie (Thessaly), we gave three eyes to Jupiter. We said that Laomedon, and then the King Priam, had fact to place this statue of Jupiter in one court, the middle of their Palace: it is this that Virgil we learn by this description:

AEdibus in means, vault under echeris ax
Great altar was, next to the ancient laurels
Kneeling are, illumined umbra complex Homes.
Virgil. Aeneid, Book II.

The middle of palace of Priam, and without any other blanket than that of sky same, the there to have a grand altar, close whose one raised a laurel very old, supported against the altar, and who concealed of his shadow the Gods tutelary of this palace.

When Troyes (Troy) was surprise by the Greeks, Priam, accompanied of Hecube (Ἑκάβη)(Hekábē) his wife, and of his girls, is was refugee towards this even altar, embracing the simulacrums of the Gods it invoked vainly, because the there was massacre of the hand of Pyrrhus.

Stenebus, son of Capaneus, fit carry then this statute to Lariffe (The raffle). Gold, what than is the artist who to fact this figure, I think that the three eyes that there remark make the symbol of the triple power of Jupiter: of two he regard the earth and the sea, and of third he regard the sky.

We representative the King Lysimachus with one horn the forehead, by one Taurus that Alexandre was ready of sacrifice, having broken his connections, and having escaped, this King seizing the Taurus by the horn, stopped him with his two hands, and the brought the place of sacrifice.

We put one star as the forehead of Julius Caesar, by that preview, they say, one comet in the sky the day it was killed in full Senate.

We represent Marcus Brutus with a small hat and two small daggers, by that, the day of his formed, the people ran by the village, a hat as the head (the hat is the emblem of the freedom) and it appeared than the daggers whose had served Brutus and Cassius, were the instruments who had recovered the freedom in Rome.

The Romans had custom of join and of dedicate together, in their gymnasium or colleges, the statute of Mercury and of Minerve: Ciceron the called *Hermathenes*, it is to say, statute of Mercury and of Minerve, asked placed on a same pedestal. (Letter of Ciceron to Atticus, book I, letter.2.). This that you write me (he said) the subject of your Hermathene, made me the more grand pleasure: it is an ornament very suitable to our Academy, by that Hermes is common to all the science, and that this Academy is devoted particularly to Minerve.

Gold the Hermatbenes resemble the other statues of Hermes; they were of the pedestals rather that of the statues, whose the heads cater himself change; and when there placed the two heads of Mercury and of Minerve, attachments together, we the appetite Hermatbenes: this name being compose of two words greeks, Ερμης Mercury Αθηνη (Athene's) Minerva.

Of the colossus the more famous.
For the boldness of the grandeur of the figure, there is in at of the examples countless, since we see that to imagine of the masses enormous of statues call colossal, who are being equal to of the towers. Such is the Apollo the Capitol, brings of the villa of Apollonia in the Pont, by M. Lucullus. He at thirty cubits of high, and at cost 500 talens (1). Such is the Jupiter of field of Mars, dedicated by Cl. Caesar, and that called Pompeyen (Popeye), looks it is close of theater of this name. Such is that of Tarente (Tarento), fact by Lysippe (Lysippos): he at forty cubits. This it there at surprising it is that, by the rightness of his balanced, we can (they say) the move to the hand, without however no hurricane can the reverse.

(1). Two million three hundred fifty thousand livers. (deliver.) franc, weight of money values.

We said that the artist to accused this inconvenience, in opposing one column to little of distance of the statue, of side or it fallout principally to break up the wind. The grandeur and the difficult of the move have preclude Fab. Verrucosus of there to touch, when he to transport of same place the Hercules who is the Capitol.

The most admire of all the colossus was that of Sun to Rhodes; he to have summer by Chares of Linde, high of Lysippos; this figure to have seventy cubits of height. She was overturned, fifty-six years after, by a tremor of earth: but all shot that she is, we not know keep from of the admire. He there at little of men who can embrace his thumb: his fingers make more grand than the mostly of the statues: the empty of his limbs broken resemble to the aperture of vast cavern. We see inside stone of one size extreme, whose the weight the firming was her based. We said that she was twelve years to make, and that she cost 300 talens (I), who knew the price of the procurement that the King Demetrius to have abandon in front of the villa, when he in up the siege, bored of its length. *Pline, book. XXXIV, Chapter. VII, section. XVIII.*

(I) One million four hundred ten thousand (livers) Franc. (Weight of coins)

This colossus remained beaten down as he was without that there should touch, pendant 894 years, the end about whom, the year of Jesus-Christ 672, Moawias, the fixth Chalice or Emperor of the Sarrafins (Sarrasins), having taken Rhodes, the selling to a Merchant Jewish, who in had the charge of nine hundred camels; that is to say, that in spot eight hundredweight for one charge, the brass of this statue, after the waste of so of years by the rust, and etc., and of this who in all likelihood in to have summer stolen, himself assembly tool again to seven hundred twenty thousand pounds, or to seven thousand two hundred quintals. Prideaux, part II, book. II.

He there to encore in the same villa hundred other colossus more small, but who suffice each for illustrate the village or they Faroese. Outraged those ones, he there at five giants of Gods, made by Briaxis.
The Italian to produce also of the giants (colossus): because we see in the library of temple of August, the Apollo Tuscan, who to fifty feet since the thumb, and in which we in fact this who is the more admirable or of bronze, or of labor.

Sp. Carvilius, with the breastplates, the helmets, and the armor of legs of the Samnites defeated, was known to a Jupiter who is Capitol. Her grandeur is such that we the view of the place or is the Jupiter Latiarius (Latiaris). Of the filing of this statue he fit make his, who is the feet of that of God. Two heads the same Capitol attract the admiration: they have summer consecrated by the Consular P. Lentulus: the one is done by Chares, whose have spoken more high; the other by Decius. But that of latter loses so to the comparison, that she appears the work of an artist absolutely fans merit.

But of our time, Zenodore (Zenodorus) to surpass all the grand figures of this species by a Mercury that he to fact in one village of the Gaules (Gaul) in Auvergne. She was ten years to make, and hearkened 400000 small Sesterce (Sestertius) (I). After than this artist had enough was acquainted his talent in this country, he was call to Rome by Neron, who he fit the statue giant of hundred ten feet of height. She was then devoted under the sun, the crimes of this prince having fact to hate her memory.

(I) Four hundred thousand pounds.

We admired in his workshop the resemblance perfect not only in the of figure of clay who was the model of the work, but again in the small models or splinters who had served of studies for the grand. This statue fit view that the art of to melt the bronze was lost, because Neron was willing to do not spare the gold and the money, and Zenodore was not inferior to none of the ancient Statuaires for the science of shape and of to repair. When was her statue in Auvergne, he copy for Vibius Avitus, Governor of the Province, two vases chiseled of the hand of Calamis, whose Caesar Germanicus, who the loved a lot, fit present to Cassius Silanus, uncle of Avitus, his preceptor. The copy was if exact that to sentence could we perceive some difference in the labor. So, more Zenodore was clever, more he is easy of see that we to have lost the art of to melt the bronze (I). Pline. After of the section XVIII above.

The plate. XXXIII, and XXXIV, XXXV and XXXVI, offer the representation of diverse heads characterized, for of the statues more grand than the natural.

The plate. XXXVII contains four heads of Athenians in different attitudes, from of the ancient monuments.

(I) To see the reputation of this absurdity of Pliny, in one of the notes that M. Falconnet to added to her translation of the weights XXXVI, XXXV, and XXXVI of this Author, printed in Amsterdam in 1772, in-8°. page 41.

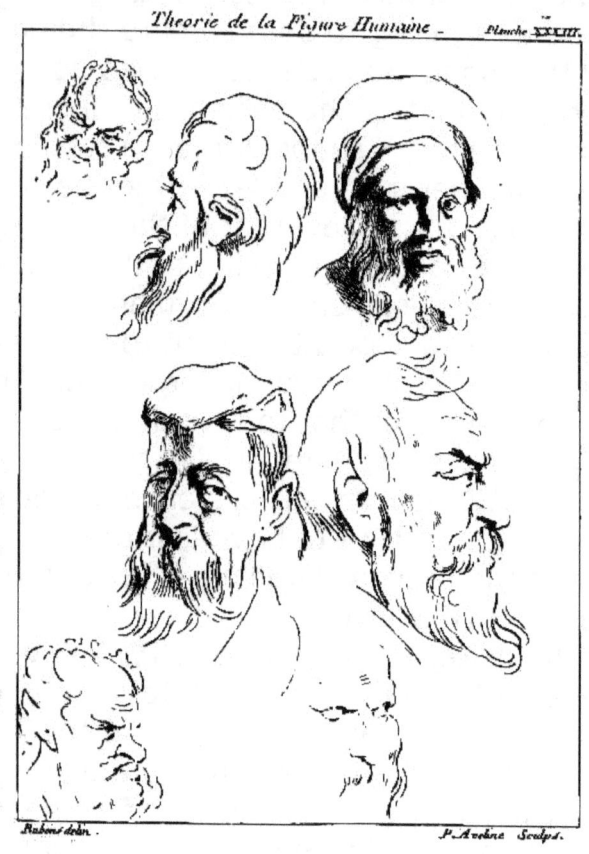

Theorie de la Figure Humaine — Planche XXXIII.

Rubens delin .   P. Avebne Sculps.

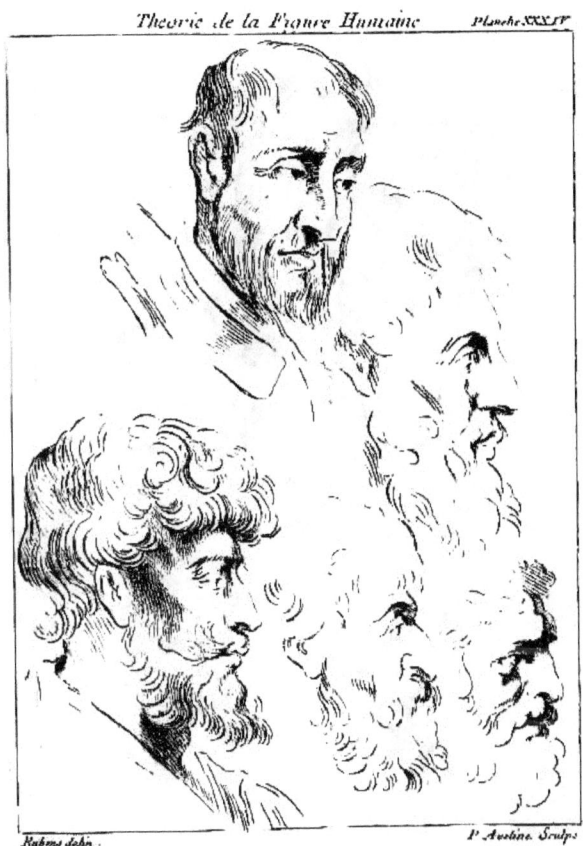

Rubens delin.   P. Aveline Sculps

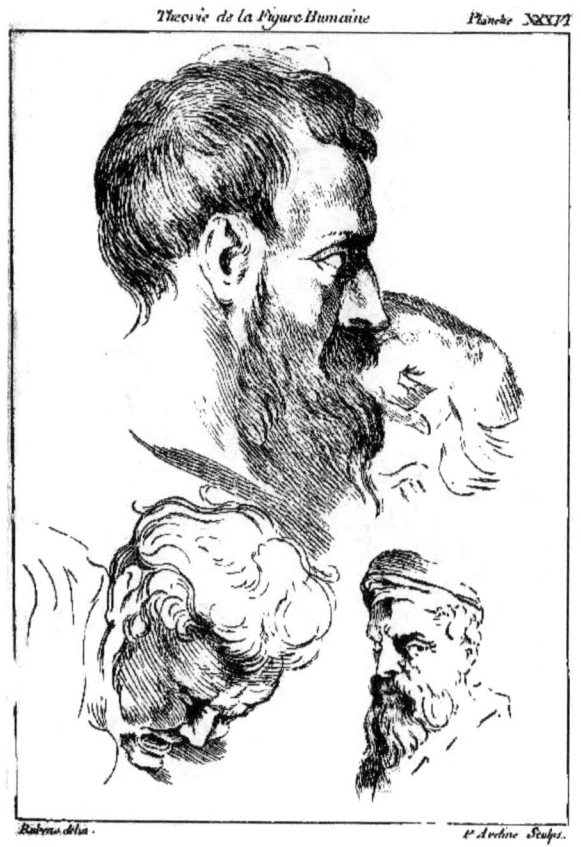

Rubens delin.   P. Arcline Sculps.

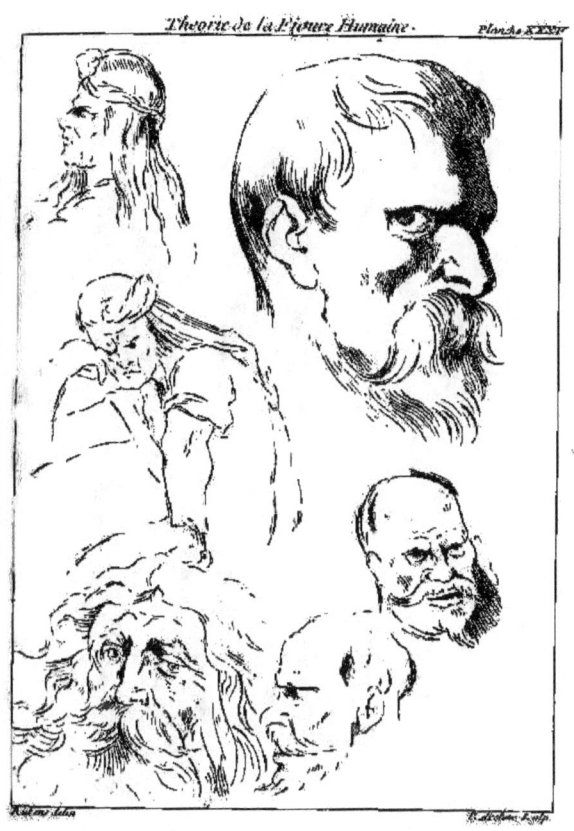

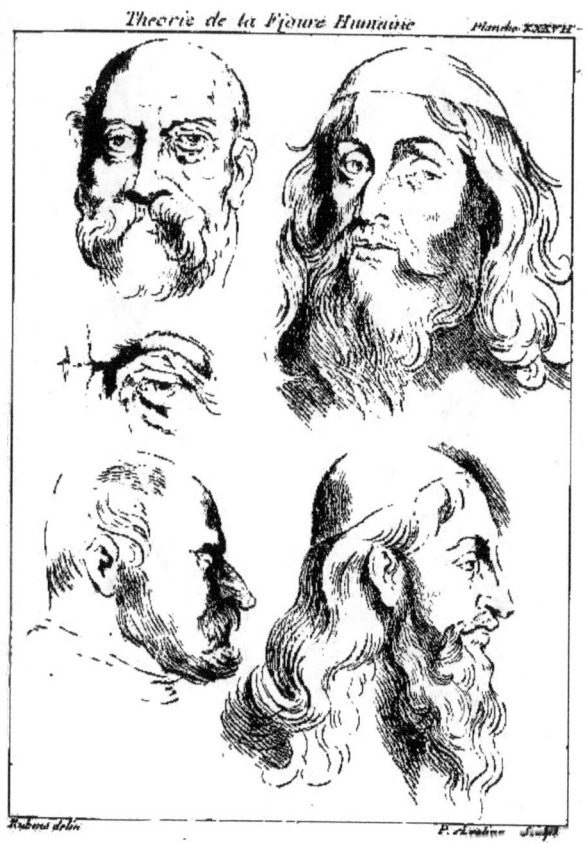

Rubens delin.   P. Aveline   sculp.

Chapter VI. (6)
Some statues of children.

Among the models of statues who we remain of the antiquity, he must always to choose the bets, and imitate in each this who appropriate the better at each age. For the childhood, by example, we in have an example very left in these geniuses children who himself see around of the statue of Nil (Nile), in the gardens of Vatican: they make round and delicate, in of the attitudes frolicsome and light-hearted, the each crawling for so say to earth, the other if striving of mount as the grands limbs and as the body of their father, such as one high Mountain. The childhood than is sees nearby of the statue of Tibre (Tiber), breastfed by one wolf, make in the same character.

The ancient we have leash an example of an age a little more advanced, but however again babyish, in the Cupid dormant layer as the cast of a lion taking a torch of her hand left.

The children which is we sees to side of the statue of Leda, who play with a swan, and the Hercules child who muffled a serpent, being again the cradle, make of the model of one age superior precedence.

Finally we to a model of children of an age still more advanced, in the young Greek who himself mingled in the combats of Ceste (Cestus).

All these various characters of children, who have again the overweight and the size limbs of the childhood, himself see to Rome as the marbles ancient.

The small children have to himself represent with of the movement prompts, and of the contortions of body when they are seated. Being standing, they have to appear fearful and timid. *Leon. of Vinci, Chapter LXI.*

All the small children have the joints unbound, and the spaces who make entre two more large: this arrive by that it are it as the joints than the single skin, without other fleshiness that of one nature nerve, which attached and dregs the bone together, and all the flesh wheel and full himself find entre the one and the other joints locked entre the skin and the bone. But by than in the joints the bone take more large than entre the same joints, it flesh, at measure that the man believes, just to let this redundancy who remained entre the bone and the skin, one good that the skin if approaches more near of the bone, and just to return the limb more hairlines around of the joints, by that are having point there of cartilages and of skin nervous, it not can himself wither, and without drying it not decreases point. Of strong that, by these reasons, the small children make weak and fleshless the joints, and far entre the same joints, as he appears to their fingers, the arms the shoulders they have slender, hollow, and long. But all the contrary a men is large and knotty all over the joints of the arms and of the legs; and the place than children them have hollow, thereof them have identified. Leon. Of Vinci, Chapter. CLXVIII.

Entre them men and them children I find one grand difference of length of the one to the other joints, of as much that the men to since the joints of the shoulders until elbow, of elbow the end of thumb, and of the extremity of one shoulder to the other one width of two heads: to the children this width it is that of one head; by that the nature grid on firstly to the composition of the principal piece, who is the seat of the understanding, rather than to this who concerned only the minds vital. Leon. Of Vinci, Chapter. CLXIX. See them different figure of children represented as the plate XXXVIII.

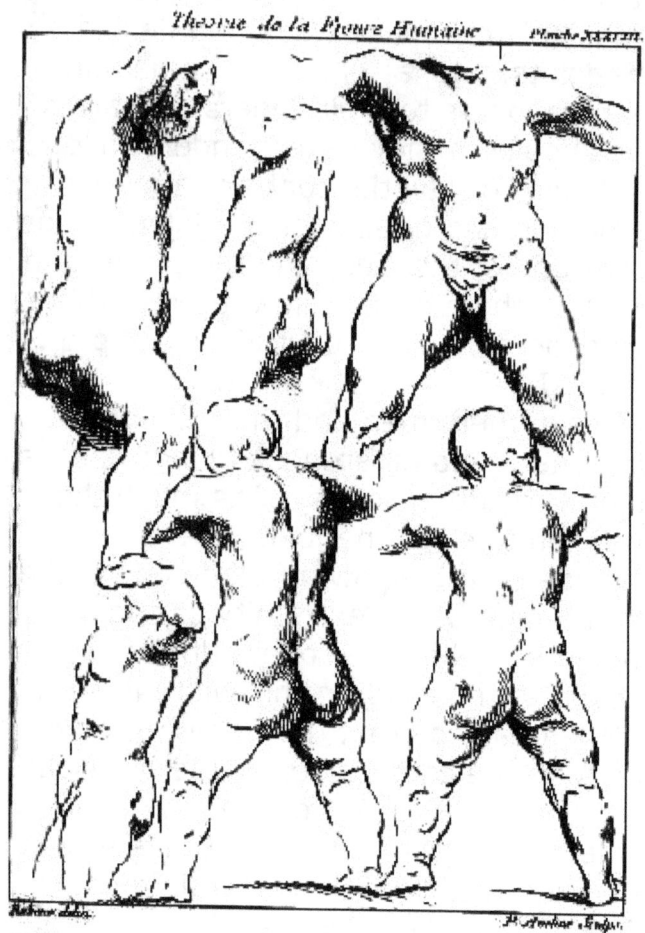

Chapter VII.
Of the proportions of the female.

The circle, or the figure circular, dominate in the form of the female: Plato assures that it is the figure the more beautiful (1). The circle and the form rounded make his elements primitive, and make the cause and the principle of all beauty: as in the man the cube and the square make them elements of the force, of the grandeur, and of the size. Them element of the figure human are different in the man and in the female, in this that in the man all the elements tend to the perfection, as the cube and the triangle equilateral: in the female, the contrary, all himself find more weak and more small. From where he arrives that, in the female, the perfection is lesser, but the elegance of the forms is more grand: the place of cube who is weakened in the figure of the female, it is a square-long or parallelogram rectangle, whose them sides are uneven; and the place of triangle it is one pyramid: the place of circle, it is an oval. Of the, we can infer that, for the perfection of the form, the women is holding the second rank after the man, being more prone that him to the predestination: the form of the man

(I) See the citation Latin about Cicéron (Cicero), page 6.

not to so need of any other animal, but she is built as his own principles: the idea of the beauty of the man having summer created perfect, as he is very probable that she to exist primarily in Adams and in the Christ.

Of the perfection of the diverse parties of body of the female.

Here is the models of beauty that them skilled artists, is Painters or Sculptors, have determine for the bodies of the female. He must, according to them, that she is of one stature poor, that she not falls point in the default of be or too much small, but that she yours a just middle, with one proportion elegant in his limbs, accordance the examples that we have left the old Sculptors Greek.

The bodies not must be or too much slim or too much skinny or too much large or too much or fat, but of one overweight moderate, following the models of the statues ancient.

The flesh solid, grange, and white, color of one red-pale, as the colors who participate of milk and of blood, or formed by a mixed of lily and of pink.

The face gracious, who not is disfigured by any wrinkled: the collar a little length, fleshy, fact the tower, of a white of snow, cleared, and without no hair.

The shoulders poorly wide: the arms round and calves: the hand long and fleshy, the fingers elongated and flexible, who himself fold and himself bow for to touch with lightness.

The chest united and ample, with a little of elevation: the nipples or breasts softly separated, round, point flabby or floppy, flaw in moderation as the chest. The waist towards the belt have to be more narrow than the high of body, sprain that this part has one form triangular.

The fold of the hips, the hip or the high of the thigh, and the thigh themselves have to be wide and ample.

The skin of belly born must not enter loose, or the belly pending, but calf and of a contour meek and flowing since her more great projection until low of belly. The part natural small and identified.

The part of back who is enter the two armpits must be flat, a little down in the middle, and fleshy, ensure that there as a furrow the long of the spine of back, and that we noticing to sentence the contour of the shoulders.

The buttock round, fleshy, of a white of snow, rolled up, and point of all pending. The thigh swollen, mostly of side or it himself joint the buttocks: the knee fleshy and round.

The leg must be right, whose the fat fault with elegance, done the tower from in decreasing with grace, as one pyramid, until heel. The feet small and well proportion, with one growth fleshy as the part higher called instep. Born you weary point, said Ovide (Ovid), of praise the grace of his face, the beauty of his hair, the delicacy of his fingers, and the smallness of his feet.

Neither face, neither you regret praise hair, and patents fingers, demanded that foot. Ovid

In a word, in the figure of the female, he must observe that his features or the contours of his muscles, her way of himself to pose, of walk, of sit, all his movement and all his actions are representing of way that we are noticing nothing who yours of the man; but that accordance to his element primitive, who is the circle, she is entirely round, delicate, and flexible, and entirely opposed to the form robust and virile.

At the beauty of the forms and of the contours delicate of the female, he must add a lot of modesty, and one grand simplicity and equality in her capacity. He must mostly to avoid with care, is in his limbs, is in his attitudes, all stiffness and appearance of muscles. Finally, when wife is standing, the distance of a foot to the other, and when she is seated, the spacer of his thighs have to be adjusted following the rules of the beneficence, in the reason of the pyramid who presided the actions of the female, of as much more than the pyramid overturned is also the hieroglyphic of the female, of same than the cube dominated in the actions of the man; from where he follows that in the different attitudes of this latest, is standing, is seated, his legs and his feet make always apart the one of the other.

We observed that the same figure born dominated point in the actions and in the form of the limbs; because the pyramid corresponds to all this who constitute the man, in this that all his parts higher make more wide that the inferior, as the shoulder, the back the chest, and etc: but the cube presided to his actions. The contrary, the form oval preside to the figure of the female, by that the roundness and the elongation himself notice in all his limbs: but the pyramid presided to his actions, as we just of the note.

He must that the female are represented in of the actions deductions and full of modesty, the knees tight, the arms collected together, the head humbly inclined, and leaning a little of side. Leon. Of Vinci, Chapter. LXIV.

The females and the youth people, he born befits no good of be in of the actions or the legs are apart and too much open, by that this capacity appears haggard and too much shameless: but the contrary the legs and the thighs railway testify of the modesty. Leon. Of Vinci, Chapter. CCLIX.

We see as the plate XXXIX that the beauty of nose human is imitated of that of horse, which is straight and drawn, very little fleshy, and whose the bones are experienced: the nostril is evenly grand, long, round, and portion in the one and in the others.

Sure the plate XL we fact one comparison of the mouth human with that of horse: and the we there see that the lip of over advanced a little more than that of beneath, and that the distance who himself find entre the nose and the mouth is fate short to the one and to the other.

The plate XLI offer diverse figures of chest of the female erect, or the we can see that his attitude naturally is of to have the legs and the thighs railway the one contra the other, accordance the precepts above. We see as the plate XLII of others examples of the even rule in various figure of female standing.

We to given as the plate XLIII many figure of women standing and covered of draperies, of after a few statues antique.

The Plate XLIV is a Bacchanale (tumultuous dance. loud debauchery.) in the taste antique, of the composition of Rubens.

He had summer to desire that Rubens had known the application of the precepts above as the proportions of body of the man, and of that of the female, at of the examples choose drawn in the nature: but as he not in fact any mention in his book, we will supply to this omission of her part, in giving in a second volume, servant of supplement to this one, a Collection of studies of diverse parts of bodies human, and of academies entries draw of after nature, which we will to have appeal.

We finish this work by a precept drawn of the art of painting of Alphonse Dufresnoy.

We can, he said, in the painting commit of the mistakes of all kinds of manners; similar the trees of one forest, they himself multiply to the infinite, and among the amount of paths who can mislead, he not if in find that one alone who lead the goal. Of same that in the grand number of lines that one can pull of a point to one other, he not there in to that one straight, all the other are more or less curves according to that they if in divert more or less. For if in to guarantee, he must imitate the beautiful nature, as the have practice the ancients, and in make a favorable choice, following that the subject that one himself propose of represent the demand.

Errors it is many forest, Manifold ways, well behavior border one.
Line right like one is and is and & one thousand curved.
But by one's side ancients nature rival beautiful, what form thing own, object requires.

End.

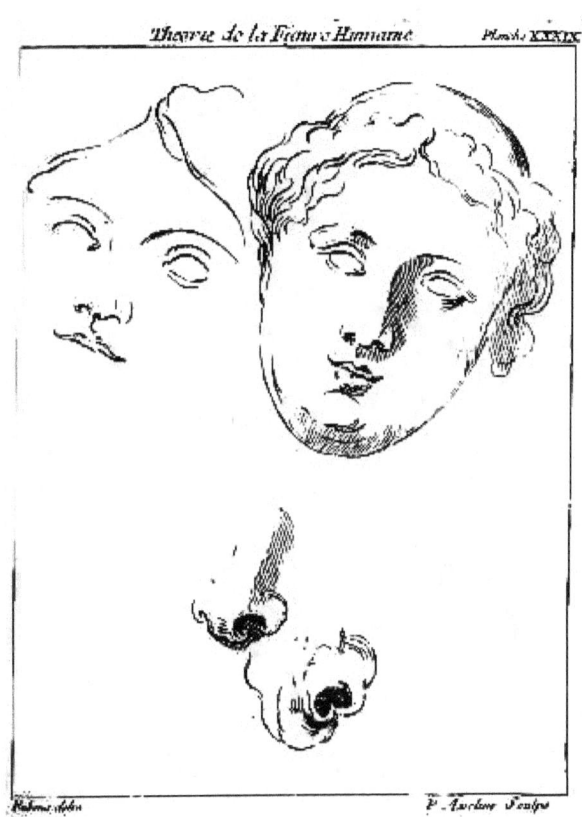

Rubens delin   P. Aveline Sculps

123

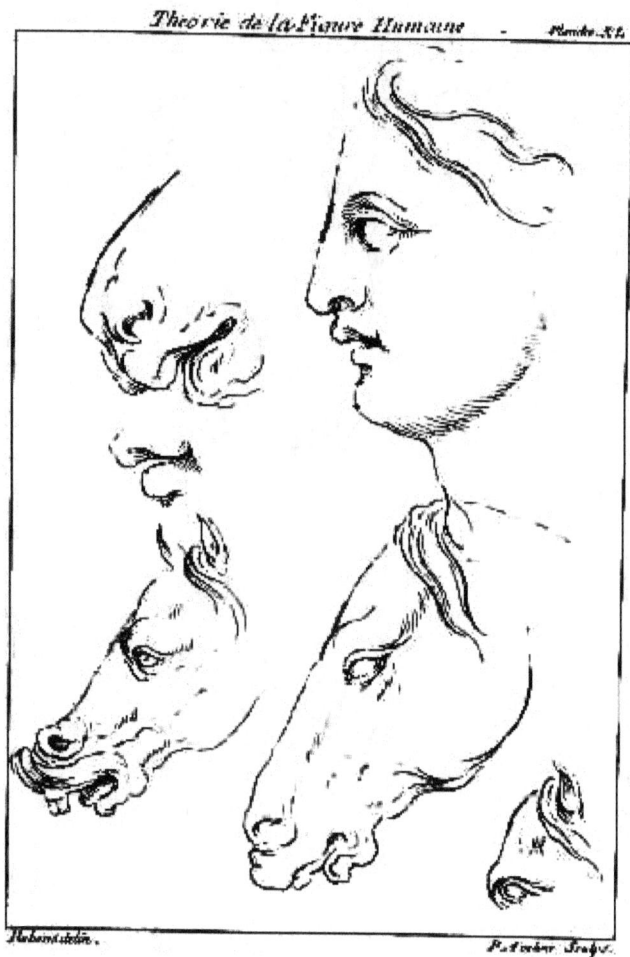

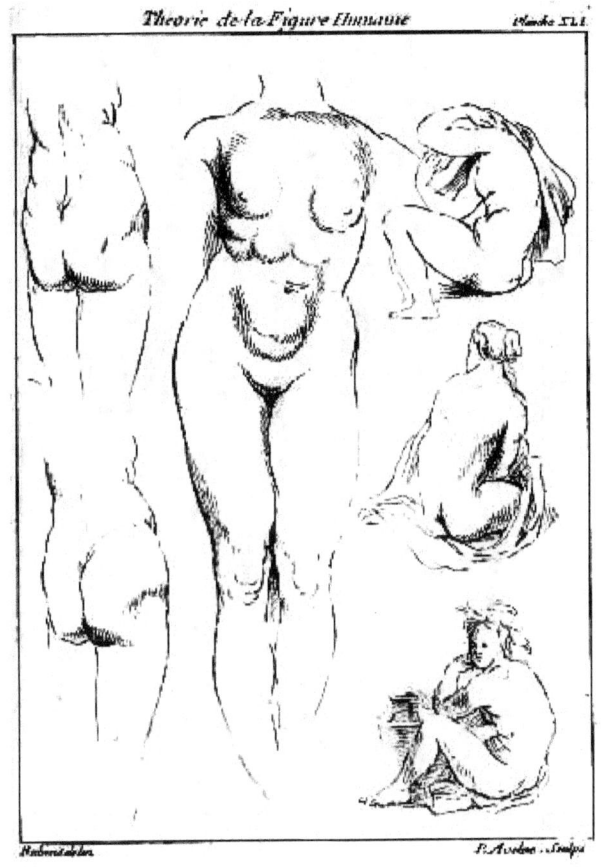

Natoire del.   P. Aveline Sculps.

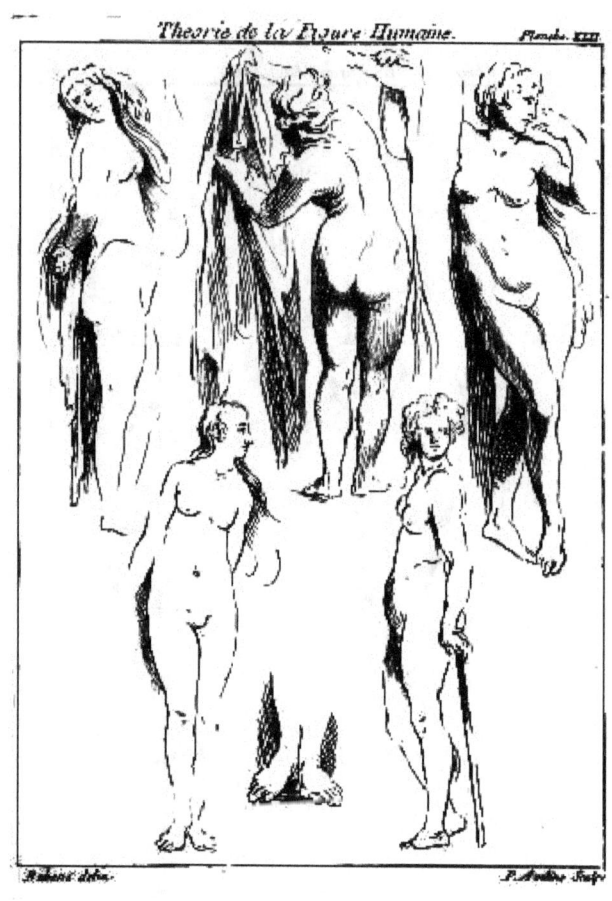

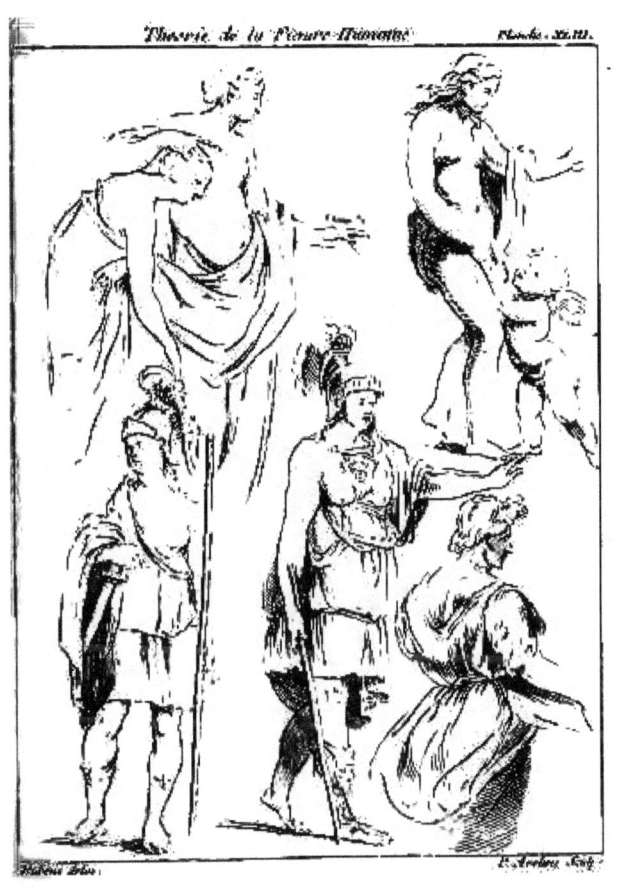

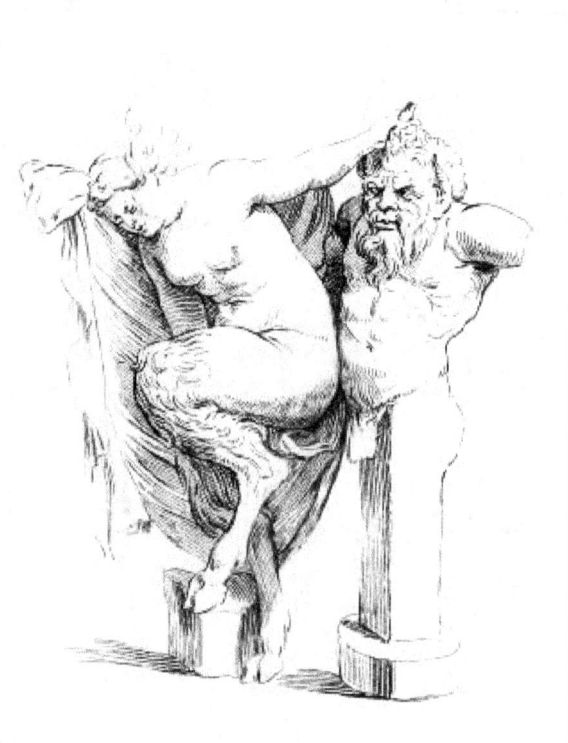

128

APPROVAL.

I have read for order of Monseigneur the Chancellor a manuscript who to for title: *Theory of the figure human*, with forty-four plates; he not contain nothing who me parish duty in prevent the impression. To Paris, this 3 July 1773. The STUTTERER OF PRESLE.

PRIVILEGE OF THE KING.

Louis, by the grace of God, King of France and of Navarre: To our souls and pail Counselor the People taking our Course of Parliament, Masters of the Queries ordinary of our Hotel, Advice Superiors, Provost of Paris, Bailiffs, Officer Royals, their Lieutenant Civils, and other we Justices that he be: Welcome. Our soul the Mr. Jombert, Father, we to fact exhibit that he desirous make to print and give the Public a Work entitled: *Theory of the figure human; Catalog reasoned of the works from Sebastien the Clerk,* if he we would please him accord our Letters of permission for this necessary. To This Cause, wanting favorably treat the Exhibitor, we him have permit and allow by these Present, of make print said Works as much of time than good him appear, and of the make sale and debit all over our Kingdom pendent the time of three years consecutive to count of day of the date Presenters. Perform defenses to all Printers, Bookstores, and other people of a few quality and condition that they are of in introduce of impression foreign in no place of our obedience; to the charge that these Present will recorded all the long as the register of the Community of the Printers and Bookstores of Paris, in three of the dated of hereunto. That the impression said Works will be done in our Kingdom, and not elsewhere, in beautiful paper and beautiful characters; that the Recipient himself accordance to in all the Regulation of the Bookstore, and especially to that of 10 April 1725, to sentence of decline of the present Permission; that before of the exhibit in sale, the manuscript who will have served of copy to the impression said Work, will handed in the same state or the approval there will have summer given, Bachelor hand of our very expensive and seal Knight Chancellor Guard of the Seals of France the Sir of Maupeou, that he in will be then handed two copies in our Library public, one in that of our castle of Louvre, and one in that of said Sir of Maupeou; the

all to sentence of nullity of the Presents:
of contents which you mend and enjoin of
make enjoy said Exponent and his
successor in fully and peacefully, without
suffer that he there is fact no trouble or
preclusion. Want to that to the copy of the
Present, who will printed all the long the
commencement or to the end of said
Works, faith is added as to the original.
Let's order the first our Bailiff or Sergeant
as this required, of make, for the
execution of hereunto, all acts required
and necessary, without demander other
permission, and notwithstanding clamor of
hark, Charter normal and Letters to this
constraint. Because such is our pleasure.
Given to Companion the fourth day of
month of August the year one thousand
seven hundred seventy-three (1773), and
of our reign the fifty-eighth, by the King in
his Council, The (Begue.) STUTTERER.

Registered in the Register XIX of the
Chamber Royal and Syndical of the
Booksellers and Printers of Paris. N°.
2465, folio 120, accordance the
Settlement of 1723. To Paris, this 13
August 1773. C A. JOMBERT, father,
Trustee.

After of the theory of the figure Human.

Second Part,

CONTAINING THE PRINCIPLES OF DESIGN.

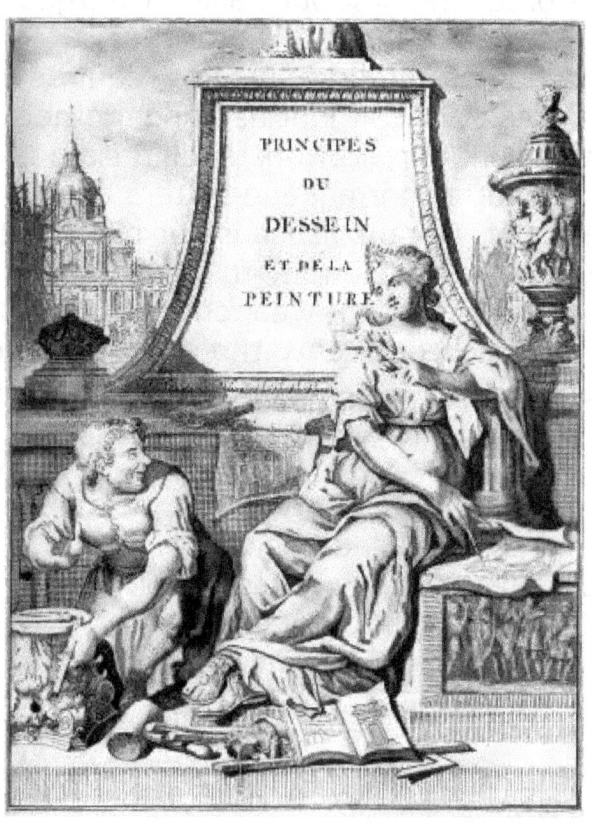

PRINCIPLES OF DESIGN,
APPLIED TO THE PRACTICAL.

Whither the we find quantity of examples of all the parts of body human, several figures of Academies, different subjects very varied, own to form the taste, and various scenery; the all of after the best Masters of the School Françoise Modern.

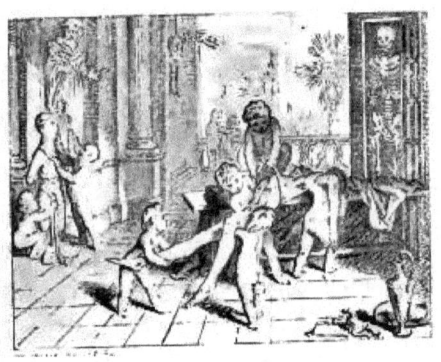

To Paris, Street Dauphine,
Amongst CHARLES - ANTOINE JOMBERT,
Father, Bookseller of King for the Artillery and the Genius.

========================

M. DCC. LXXIII.

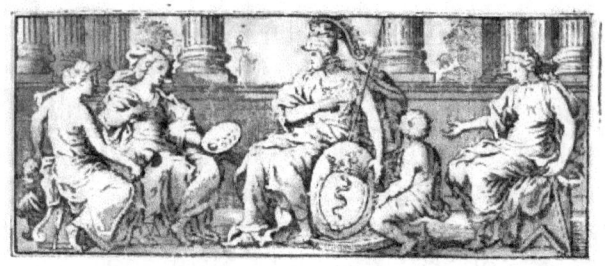

Principals of design, Applied to the Practice.

Of design, and of the manner of the to study.

Short of we stop the different definitions of design than the we to give so far, whose the mostly make more curious and sought that instructive, we say that it is the art of imitate the form of the object who himself present to our eyes. The design is the foundation of the painting, he in is the part the more essential, for those who himself destinc to this noble profession. We not would have so if there take too much early for in learn the first element, of as much more than in the age the more tender, the hand again docile himself ready more easily to the flexibility than required this kind of work.

For reach to good draw, he is necessary of to have of the justified in the bodies that we there employee, and of the there form by one long and continual habit.

All the convenient of the art of design himself reduced to three things; known, the design of after the studies of the grand Master, that who himself fact of after the hump, and the design of after the model living, or of after nature We will itemize these three manners in the articles following.

Of design of after the studies of the grand Masters.

The first drawings that we give to copy the youth are facts ordinarily, of after nature, by a clever Master. The plate 2 of this collection represent of the ovals of head views of face, of three quarters, of profile, lifted, lowered, and etc. It is over there that one high must commence: he must if exercise to the trace a crayon until to this that he in has grasped the divisions and the lines on which make poses the eyes, the nose, the mouth the ears, and ect: by than it is of this principle good designed that the we succeed to put together one head, in some situation that it himself find. He copy then all the parts of the head, taken separately, represented as the plates 3, 4, 5, and following, who offer a choice of studies make by the more clever artistes of the Academy Royal of Painting and of Sculpture, very-own for serve of models to those who want if instruct in the art of design. These twelve first plates are engraved by M. Pasquier, of after MM. Dandré Bardon and Boucher. He there to five plates of eyes in all kind of positions, three plates of ears, and two of nose, and mouths: we not can see of better express, or of more proper to form the taste and the hand of the youth people.

The students will pass then the heads whole, in making usage of the principals the he just of t copy; that is to say, for example, that he must as attention that the lines as which make seats the eyes, the nose, the mouth, and the ears, are parallel enter them, and that, whatever these lines born are point traces as the original that he to in front of him, this principle are is not less observe exactly. Of after these considerations, he commences by sketch or draw slightly the altogether of the head; in comparing the parts the one the others, and the distances who the separate, he reviews if his design is conform to the original. So he will give more of firmness to this together; that is to say, that he will further this that it just of sketch: then he there adds to the shading, in following exactly his original. He establishes of on board the principal's masses of shading, that he softens towards the light for of the halftones, in loading less of crayon his design. He to compare to also the parts shaded the one the others, the halftones the reflections, and the reserve his last stroke of crayon for the touch the more strong.

The high continue to copy of the drawings of head views of different sides, until this that he himself is enough Familiarity with these first principles for it conformer well-passably. He draws then of the feet and of the hands, of the arms and of the legs; we in will find of the examples as the twelve plates following, since the n°. 13 till and including the n0. 24. They are engraved by the same M. Pasquier, of after the design of celebrated Bouchardon, and of MM. Lemoine, Boucher, and Natoire, three of the more clever Painters of our school modern, whose the name alone worth a praise.

After this studies repeated, the elevated copy of the design of academies, or figures whole; but previously he must learn to in cognize the proportions general. In beginning his design. He if attach to by grab the tower or the movement of the figure who him serves of models, in the sketching slightly the crayon. He observer as this model the parts who himself correspondent perpendicular and horizontal, to of the put each to their place, the one to the respect of the other. Relief by the proportions that he knows already, he himself conforms to those of design that he copies; that is to say, the proportions reciprocal and the report of all the parts with the figure entire. Finally when believeth be as of all these things, he strengthen the contours of her figure, in there giving all the finesses of detail, the character, and the lightness of the original. He shows the forms external and exposed, caused by the position indoor of the muscles, the masses of shadow and of light. It is this that the we call to put together or the feature one figure. So he will end his design, that is to say, that he the ombrera (shadow covering), as we have said above, in observant the comparison of the shading with the halftone and the reflections of design original.

He must trade for establish slightly all the masses of shadow, to of power the carry little by little the thy of those of his example, in himself referring for the end of give the forces and the touches the more vigorous. We spare the reflects, and the we strengthen the locations who not in receive point; we will be good attention the halftones who bind the lights the shading of one way insensitive, and who prevent the shading of to slice. Finally the we follow of point in point this that we to under the eyes; because to copy a design, it is the imitate of such way that the we can take the copy for the original. For this effect, he must if exercise to many occasions as different designs of heads, feet, hands academies, and figure whole of men, of women, and of children, of figure drape, and etc.

We can draw indifferently, is the crayon (pencil) of sanguine [1] or of stone red as of paper of halftone, grey, blue, or color of flesh tender, that the we fabricated express for the draughtsman: all these ways of draw recur the same. If, for example, we draw as of paper of halftone, the tone of paper form naturally the halftones, and the we warm the lights with the crayon white: by consequent, we charge less his design of crayon of sanguine, [1] or of stone black, for form the shadows.

1.(variety of orange pulp red.)

The contrary, when draws as the paper white, the more strong lights are formed by the paper same: we is oblige of make the halftones with the crayon of color, and the we charge the shading to proportion, following his original.

For the study than we just of prescribe, the high will acquire this sharp eye just, this habit and this ease to manner the crayon that the we appointed practical, who have to be the principal object of his study, and of time that he there employ, if he wants make some progress in the art of design.

We give in the III^0 after (who contains the twelve plates since the n^0. 25 until n^0.36), twelve figures of academies design of after nature, and engraved for the mostly by the more clever Master of the Academy; know, MM. Bouchardon, Collin of Vermont, Tremolieres, Carie Vanloo, Boucher, and Natoire. The fourth after contains twelve other plater of academies, since the n^0. 37 until n^0. 48 design likewise of after nature, and in part engraved for the same Academicians: the other plate of figure of academies are engraved by MM. Cochin father, Aveline, Perronneau, and Soubeyran, all excellent Engravers, who themselves are attached to good return the mind who fact the merit of the drawings original. These part can be placed enter the hands of the youth student for the copier, in attendant they themselves find enough spells for steal of their own wings, and for to work by themselves of after the models living.

Of design of after the hump.
He there to one if grand difference entre copier a design trace as the paper, and design of after nature as one surface flat of the objects that we see of round hump, or of relief, that he not is hardly possible of pass all of one stroke of design of after the studies of the grand Masters to that of after the models. We to find a middle who aid to pass of the one to the other, it is this that we call draw of after the hump. This hump not is other thing that one object any, as head, feet, hand, or figure whole, model in earth or in wax, or of plaster throws in mold; or good it is one figure of marble, of stone, of bronze, and etc. or finally a low relief. These objects various, who have the same roundness that the nature, being private of movement, give the ease to the high, who see always her figure under the same aspect, of draw this object, in himself taking good just in the same point of view.

In the model living, the opposite, the lesser movement involuntary and almost insensitive, embarrassed the artist again novice, in him presenting often of the surfaces tidings, and of the effects of light difference.

In the studies of after the hump, the attention becomes more necessary than in that of after the drawings; and the difficulties that the high experiences become more grands. He must that he reasons and that he compares this that he to fact, this that he goes make, and this that he goes see, with this that he to goes in the drawings of the Masters that he to copies so far. He must that he connoisseur the bone by their names, by their forms, and their articulations; that he connoisseur the muscles who the envelop, their origins, their insertions, their functions, and their forms, to of power give the character and the resemblance suitable the movements of the figure: it is the study of the anatomical who must the guide now. We find in Jombert an *Abstract of anatomy to the usage of the Painters,* placed the day for *Tortebat,* in a volume *in-folio,* that we believe sufficient for fill this object; we have not vintage duty in speak right here, for to avoid a double employment.

The high may to study, in this abridged of anatomy, the skeleton human who there is likewise represent, with of the letters of return for the speech of explanation who is overlooked. The fruit who results of this study the lead to draw of after the hump and then of after nature, with knowledge and discernment, and to give to all his productions a character of resemblance.

The principal figures antique that we cognize are the Hercules Farnese, the Antonius, the Apollo, the Venus of Medicis, the Laocoon, the Torso, and etc. and such of others who offer the artists the means of acquainted the beautiful and the elegance of the proportions. We them find detailed in the book entitled: Method for learn the design, by *Charles-Antoine Jombert, in fourth*. 1755, chapter. V, page 75 and following. As the young student, curious, of learn, not can himself dispense of join the lecture of the work to this one, we us dispense of in speak further. We will observer only that these masterpieces of the antiquity are of as much more precious than their Authors, in the forming, have corrected the defaults same of the nature. We append that, for the beauty of their choice, these figures reassemble each, relatively to this they represented, a one beautiful character, joined to so of graces, of elegance, an of perfection, that he would be impossible of the come up with united in one same subject animated.

Before that of design in whole these antiques, he will kindly of in design the parts separately, same head, feet hands, and etc: we will then all the figure: For the to put together, we if there will take as we have said of the academies, and the we covering area in following exactly the effect of model, and in comparing the masses of shad the reflections and the halftones. The goal of these study is of preparer the student to design of other nature, and of him make cognition the beautiful proportions and the beautiful forms.

We define of after the hump, so that of after nature, the day or good to the lamp, with such crayon (pencil) and as such paper that the we judge at propose. Before that of to start these studies of after nature, he will good of learn the perspective. We not to point judge to propose of in give the principles in this abridged, but we the will find very good demonstrated and placed to the scope of the artist, in the book who to for title:

Treaty of prospective to the usage of the artist, according to the methods of M. Sebastian the Clerk, for M. *Jeaurat* his grandson, in fourth, with a lot of figures, amongst *Jombert.*

Of design of after the model living.
We will right here the recapitulation of the acquaintances that the student must to have acquired in student the perspective, the anatomy, and the figures ancient, to of in make one just application.

The perspective is absolutely necessary the young artist for good design the plan of one figure or of one group: for express the shortcuts and the decrease of the body to measure they if hold off of the eye of spectator, and for may to put in same time of the intelligence in the masses of light and of shadow relatively the plans they occupy. The drawings of the grand Masters show clearly they had fact one study serious of this science, so that of the anatomy, they watching as the based fundamental of design. In effect, when the possesses all two, not only we if saving a lot of time and of sentence, and the we not fact nothing the hazard; but all this that the we draw of after nature, threshold with self this character of truth and of precision who hit the first sharp eye.

The perspective is again necessary for grab and make pass to propose a contour as another, to of hunt the part who follows; intelligence without which the together will be false, and with the effect the better heard, with the lights and the shading the better observed, one figure appear always ridiculous, and It will not be the action that we himself proposed: he in is of same for the groups of many figures. To the respect of finished, or of the effect, it is also the perspective who determine in general the degree of force of the shading as the first plans, and their weakening to measure that bodies who the produce if estrange. The shading brought follow this same principle; he must however there join the knowledge of effect of light that the we appointed chiaroscuro.

The knowledge of the anatomy is of one necessity indispensable for the young designer; she serves to him make acquainted the frame of bodies human, that is to say, the structure of the bone who change the form exterior of body in general, and that of each limb in particular: it him serves again for give the muscles their veritable position, and for power the express properly to the action they have as the limbs, and the movements they their printer. It is for his relief that the we mark further those who are in action, and that the we give to those who obey the movement of the other the inflections who form this beautiful contrast that the we remark in the nature.

The study thoughtful in ancient serves to correct the forms, sometimes defective, of the nature, and to himself determine as the choice of those they is more important of seize and of make feel; because in student the nature, he is to propose, in not if spreading point of the truth, of if accustom to there see principally this that she offer of grand and of noble, in there subordinating all the small parts. We must so if accustom of good hour to make this chose, for the comparison of the nature with the beautiful productions of the ancient and the works of the grand Masters.

For draw of after nature, we pose in volition a man nude, is standing, seated, or layer, or in some other attitude than this is, but however naturally; it is this that we call poser the model. He can be enlightened by the light of day, or by that of one lamp: whatever the model is beautiful to draw of all the sides, we is free however of to choose that who interested more. We define indifferently as the paper white or as that of halftone.

We must, as we the too always said in speaking of the study of after of the drawings of academies, if ally, from the first instant, to seize the tower or the movement of the figure by a feature lightweight, by than the model can himself tired and vary, mostly when looking to themselves to prepare at the art of the composition, whose an of the more grand merits is of good return the action and the movement. But when tends to himself perfection in that of good perform the detail, he is sometimes advantageous of expect, for stop his feature, that the model himself is present in some way, and that he has taken the position who him is more convenient, that we is as that he resumes always naturally; despite the notice of those who prefer of seize the first movement of the action. He in results that we to a lot of ease to study the parts who himself represent always under the same aspect. The feeling that we racy moving forward right here will of on board look opposite the lessons that give ordinarily the good Masters, it is based as the experience.

We will take so right here the same precautions that we have indicated heretofore for to put all the part good to their place, and as them plan, and the we complete of to put together its figure, in observant the proportions generals, and in showing the muscles appearance by of the contours and of the shots of crayon more insured. We will bring a lot of attention to not point to put of equality in the forms, by that the nature not in to footstep, that is to say, that one form is always balanced by one other more great or more small who the fact to be worth, of manner that the contours external not himself meet never towards the one of the others, same as of a baluster; but the contrary, they appear to avoid this get together, and if envelopment mutually. He not must that consider the nature for if in to convince.

For shade its figure, he must to start by establish his principles masses of shadow, in them giving to little near the half of tone they must have, to of power reserve the reflections of light that the model receives of the body foreign who the environment. If the we considered in general all the sides enlightened of model, we not perceive that one alone masse of light in which are of the detail occasion by the more or less of relief that have the muscles, but who born the interrupted not. So he must that all these detail, all these parts luminous are linked together of manner they not make that one all: in booking only to those who are the more projections and who receive the light the more large, the more grand clear.

In examining the nature, we if perceive that the light to this property of render sensitive all the objects of detail who are in its masse general, and that the opposite the masses of shading extinguished and confused together these same detail, to less that he not are receipts by of others object lit: of or he if follows that the shading the more deaf and the more vigorous not are by always as the first plans, but as those or he is impossible that he is brought no reflection, or good as those who are too much distant for that this light of reflection can reach enough to our eyes, and the affect enough strongly to there produce some sensation. In general, the main groups of light are always supported by the shading induce the more vigorous. We can make these observation as many figures groups together in the examples and the thumbnails of this collection, who follow the examples of figures academic then we there give.

Finally the we complete its figure in giving the shading all the force that the we will in the model, in observation of the soften of sides of the lights by of the halftones, to they not sharp point. We strengthen more the shading in the locations who not receive point of reflections. He must lean the contours of side of the lights, and give more of firmness to those who in are private. We must make also the comparison of all the parts the ones with the others, to of place to propose the lights and the keys the more vigorous, and of make feel those who advance and those who flee. By this way, we succeed to give to his design all the harmony and effect of the nature. He must mostly if to attach particularly to finish with care the head, the hands, and the feet: these parts good intended give a lot of grace to one figure, and are judge ordinarily of the capacity of designer.

We must assume custody what is this the we fact of the anatomy not results to make too much feel the muscles: It is a default in which tumble the mostly of the young people. They believe over their giving one character more masculine and more vigorous to their figures, but they themselves delude; they prove all the more that they know the anatomy. When we want express of the force and of the vigor, he must to choose a model more robust and more nervous, and the draw

Such that he is: so we will find good of the difference enter a the same design fact of after nature, and the species of flayed that we would have would have drawn of imagination. This vice is of as much more dangerous for those who himself deliver to this manner, that he there is almost impossible by the after of if subject to render faithfully the graces and the simplicity of the nature. We must so if accustom of good hour to draw the object such that we the see, in not himself serving of the lights that the we to acquired than for in judge healthily.

We will be usage of the same principles for draw of after nature the women and the children, in observant that the muscles are less appearance, this who makes the contours very flowing. We can see this that said Rubens to this subject in the first part of this work, and the examples that he thereof given, plate XXXVIII and following; but in general, when wants characterize the childhood, the adolescence, the old age, and etc, he must in make also of the studies of after nature, and make one choice resonate of the models whose we themselves serve.

Of the characters of the passions.
The expression of the passions is one
study who request a lot of application, and
that the we not must point neglect, by that
the lower compositions have one object
who oblige necessarily the designer of give
the heads of his figure the character who
their appropriate relatively the subject.
But how can draw the after nature the
various movement of the soul? How can
seize, of after one scene includes of many
people, all the sensations who them affect
each separately, following the interest
particular that they take the spectacle who
the occupied, or of hatred, or of anger, or
of despair, or of astonishment, or of
horror? When we himself proposer it of not
seize that one of these expressions, the
attempt would become almost impossible,
by that are all produced that by the
circumstances of a moment, that the
moment of after decomposed and destroy:
that is to say, that such man will pass of
an moment to the other of the hatred to
the pity, of the astonishment to the
admiration, of the joy to the pain; or that
the same passion subsistent, it himself
strengthen or if weakened, and that the
same character will take, for an observer
attentive, one infinity of countenances
successively. Here of the difficulties almost

Insuperable for the designer who himself proposer of seize with the point of his crayon of the phenomena also fugitives.

He is so very important for the young designer of make one serious attention the countenances of the characters in the different scenes of the life whose he will be witness: the images the strike, they himself engrave in his mind, and the ghosts of his imagination himself wake up the need, himself represent in front of him, and become of the models of after which he composite his subject. But for shoot an parts as and easy of the wealth of his imagination, he is necessary of to have studied previously in the drawings of Masters who them have the better rapport, the signs that they have found the more suitable for express in one head such or such passion. The young artist consult also her reason and his heart, and not will be nothing that this that he feel good himself. The celebrated the Brun, who to have studied particularly this part, we to leash of very beautiful models of these different characters of the passion, that the we can to consult. He there in to one after engraved by Audran, who himself sells to Chereau, street Saint-Jacques. Sébastien the Clerk to also serious the same characters, more in small and the simple feature, in a small booklet of twenty leaf (papers), who himself sells amongst Joullain son, Trader of prints, dock of the Mégisserie.

Of the study of the draperies.

He is very-important for the beauty of one figure that the draperies in are jetties naturally, and that the arrangement of the folds himself feel of the nature of the fabrics: so the we must, as much it is possible, the draw of after nature, and as a model living. However as this model is subject to vary, and that the lower movement can bother, if not the masse general of the draperies, of less the quantity of the folds, and their give to each moment of the forms different; he arrive of the that the designer is oblige of pass slightly as amount of small details important, for not if to attach that the play of all together and to the effect general, and that he substitute the rest in working of imagination. This disadvantage is of grand consequence, and he brings often of grand defaults of truth in a design: because he is essential, as we just of the say, that the form of the folds, their shading, and their reflections, characterize the nature and the species of the fabric, so that the we can judge if it is of washing, of sheet, of the drapery of silk, and etc. Gold, how render this who belongs to each of these species of draperies (hangings) differences, if the form of the folds, the lights, the shadows, and the reflections if vanish to each instant, and not appear never in their first state, mostly when the drapery are light and brittle?

Here is the way whose we himself serves for remedy to this inconvenience, and for to study the nature and the difference of the draperies (hangings) more conveniently: he is of a grand relief, mostly for the beginning. We throws one fabric any as one figure lifeless, but of grandeur and of proportion naturally, that the we named mannequin; he born there to not of Painter or of Designer who not the connoisseur. We pose this figure in the attitude that the we to selected: so we in define the draperies such that we the see: we can the mimics to his will in his shading, his lights and his reflection. For the comparison that the we in fact. He must reiterate this study as of the drapery differences, to of if accustom to the treat differently, by that the form of the draperies (hangings) himself support more in certain drapery, and himself interruption or himself break more or less in of others. We observed also that the

Heads of the folds are more or less pinch, and the refection more or less clear; it is to all these truths good made that the we knows that the draperies (hangings) have summer drawings of after nature.

The designer born must not ignore the way of draper of the ancient: he the acquainted in drawing of after the antiques drapes; it is a style particular who to of grand beauties, and or the we can draw the principles the more certain of the art of draper. We in will make the application in different occasions. After one long and tiresome study of after the drawings, of after the hump or the antique, and of after the nature same, if the we to of genius, we will pass to the composition.

Of the composition, and of the different manners of draw.

When the we compose a subject, we throws her first thought as the paper, to of distribute his groups of figures as of the plans who can produce an effect advantageous, by of beautiful masses of light and of shadow: this design himself named sketch. It is in consequent of this distribution and of this species of design preliminary that the we knows all the studies of figures and of draperies hangings to make for that the design is correct and finished.

We himself serves of different means for draw: they are all likewise good when they fulfill the object that is propose. We draws with the sanguine, with the stone black, with the mine of lead, to the feather, the opinion of ink of the China, and etc. For shade his design, we himself serves or of brush, or of the blur. We fact so of the drawings more or less rendering, more or less agreeable, as the sounds that we believes the more own. The pastels same of different colors serve to indicate the tone that the we to noticed in the nature. Finally, the art of draw embrace one infinity of parts, such that the effect of the muscles, the weighting of the bodies, the rightness of the action, the proportion of the parts, the purity of feature, the characters of heads, the knowledge of the ancient, the expression of the passion, the variety of the attitudes, the beauty of the groups, and etc. that he would be too much long of treat right here, and for which we can to have recourse to the *method for appended the design, by Jombert,* cites above, or good the Treaties of Paint of Leonard of Vinci, Bernard of Puy of Grez, of Piles, of Frenoy, Wattelet, Dandré Bardon, and etc.

He not is hardly possible of give the youth pupil of the examples capable of the guider in the talent of the composition this art depends of genius of designer, and of the nature of the different subjects that he himself propose of represent. However them must suit that the view of the works of the grand Masters can their heat the 'imagination and their inspire of the ideas happy. It is in this intention that after the studies of heads, feet hands, and of figures whole of academies, that the we to seen as the forty-eight first plates (boards) of this collection, we have vintage power to offer the youth students, in the forty-eight leaves following, many examples of compositions extremely varied as all kinds of subjects; the more grand part of these leaves (pics) contain of the thumbnails, florets and etc. drawn and engraved by the celebrated M. Cochin, whose the merit is so much known that his name alone fussy for excite the curiosity of the artist and of the amateurs enlightened. We there to join a few productions of many other artist in all sort of kind, whose the grand diversity not be that very advantageous for the progress of the studies of the youth draughtsman. The twenty latest leaves of this collection are of the views and of the scenery of various

Authors, among which we can to quote the famous Van Goyen, one of the more grand landscape that the Hollande has produced. This volume is completed by twelve very beautiful scenery of this artist celebrated, engraved by Jean Visscher, who will of as much more useful than this are of the views of the more beautiful locations of the Pays Bas, draw of after nature with all the accuracy and the precision than the we can to desire.

Of the study of the animals of landscape.

The art of design to for goal ordinarily of imitate the contours external, the forms and the proportions of bodies human; and it is in effect his object the more noble and the more difficult. Of elsewhere that who there successful himself find to have acquired one ease extreme for imitate the other productions of the nature, which ask however, each in his kind, one study and one attention particular.

The study of the animals must be done of after nature when wants the draw correctly and with the grace and the character who is proper to each of them; this make of the beings animated, subject to various passions, and capable of movement varied to the infinite. Their parts different of the ours in the forms, in the joins, and the fitting. It is so necessary that one Painter of history make of the studies, mostly of after the animals who himself find more related with the actions ordinary of the men, or with the subjects that he to the more often occasion of treat. He not there to nothing of if ordinary for the Painters of history that the necessity of represent of the which horses: we find however a lot to desire as this point in the works of the more clever; it is why he would be to desire that the youth artist might learn of good hour to in good know the anatomy. We can also to consult to this subject the drawings of the best Masters; but if the we himself propose some superiority in the kind particular of the animals, we not must nothing make that of after nature: it alone can drive to one imitation real, who is the goal of the art. All this who is fact of practice not in impose that the first a look; and some agreement seducer that he can present, fans the truth he not can satisfied the veritable connoisseur.

The landscape fact again one part essential of the art of draw. The freedom that give his forms undetermined might make believe that the study of the nature would be less necessary for this part; however he is if easy of to distinguish a board (picture) one sit taken as the nature, of that who not is compose that of imagination, that we not can challenge the degree of perfection that added this truth who himself fact if good sense. Of elsewhere, some fertile that is the 'imagination of an artist, he him is good difficult of not point himself repeat, if he not to recourse to the nature, who is one source inexhaustible of varieties. The draperies, the flowers the fruits, all finally must be defined, as much that he is possible, as the naturel.

Finally the art consist to see the nature such that it is, and to feel her beauties. When the feels, we can good the render, and the we possesses so this that we call the good manner: expression who suppose always the more scrupulous imitation. But this not is that for the zealous the more ardent, the study the more laborious, and the experience the more consumed than the we succeeds to this goal. The recompense is enter the hands of the artist: the cultivated his proper heritage, he sprinkles his own laurels: the flowers and the fruits who spring of this job the lead the temple of the immortality, which the desire same will be strength of him open.

We himself serves sometimes of the

chamber obscure for draw of the landscapes, of the ruins of ancient buildings, or the views perspectives. This instrument to the advantage of represent the objects such they are in the nature; of manner that those same who not know point draw, can easily represent all this they want very correctly. However when possesses the purposing, we not must point abuse of the ease that provides this instrument, in this that he cools the taste, and that this habit stop imperceptibly the progress that we might make in the art of design. We can see the description of this chamber obscure at the end of our *Method for learn the design*, edition of 1755.

The precepts and the reflections judicious content in this Abstract of principles as the design are from, for the mostly, of one speech place to the head of the plates as the design, in the third volume of collection of plates as the sciences and as the arts, making part of grand Dictionary encyclopedic. As this speech as the design himself find mingled with one infinity of others as the different arts and crafts, in one suite of twenty eight volumes *in-folio,* whose the price is become excessively among, we believe render a service essential the youth artist

in their bidder right here a extract of this
that he there to of more interesting in this
excellent speech, applied the examples
who form our collection, and rid of all this
who might be extraneous to our subject.
For render to his Author (whose we ignore
the name) the justice who him is due, we
recognize right here publicly that all this
that he there to of good in this who above
is drawn of this explanation of the plates
(boards) of the Encyclopedia, to which we
have fact the change and the additions
that we have considered necessary.

End.

Index second book part.

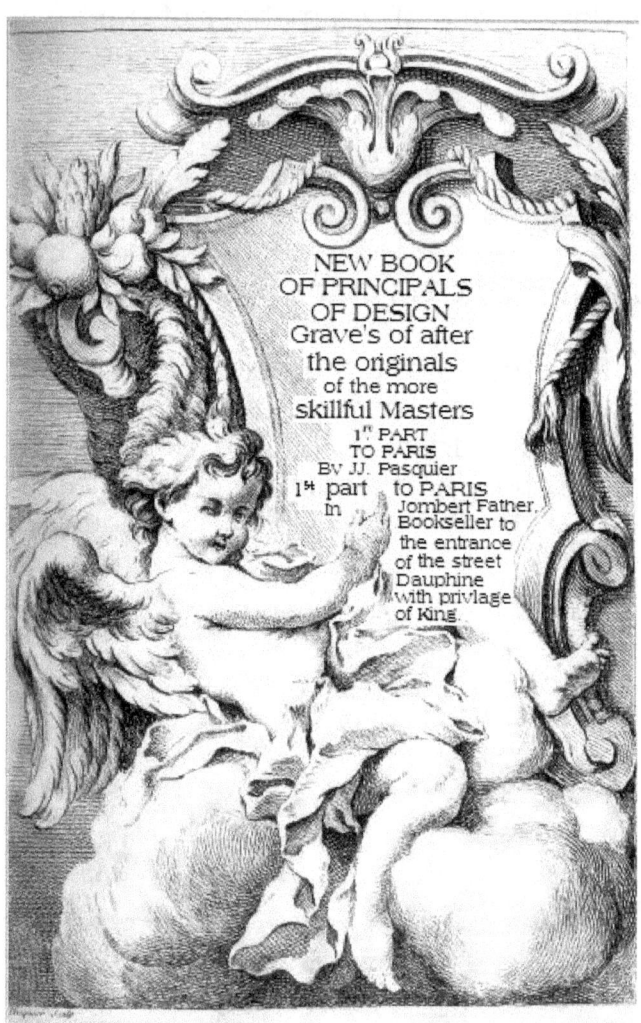

NEW BOOK
OF PRINCIPALS
OF DESIGN
Grave's of after
the originals
of the more
skillful Masters
1ⁿ PART
TO PARIS
Bv JJ. Pasquier
1ˢ part to PARIS
in Jombert Father.
Bookseller to
the entrance
of the street
Dauphine
with privlage
of King.

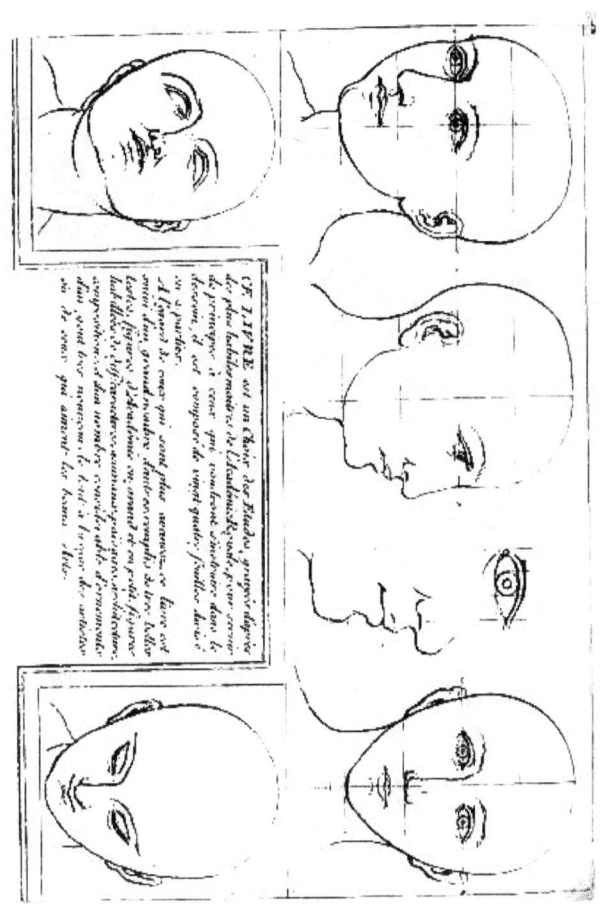

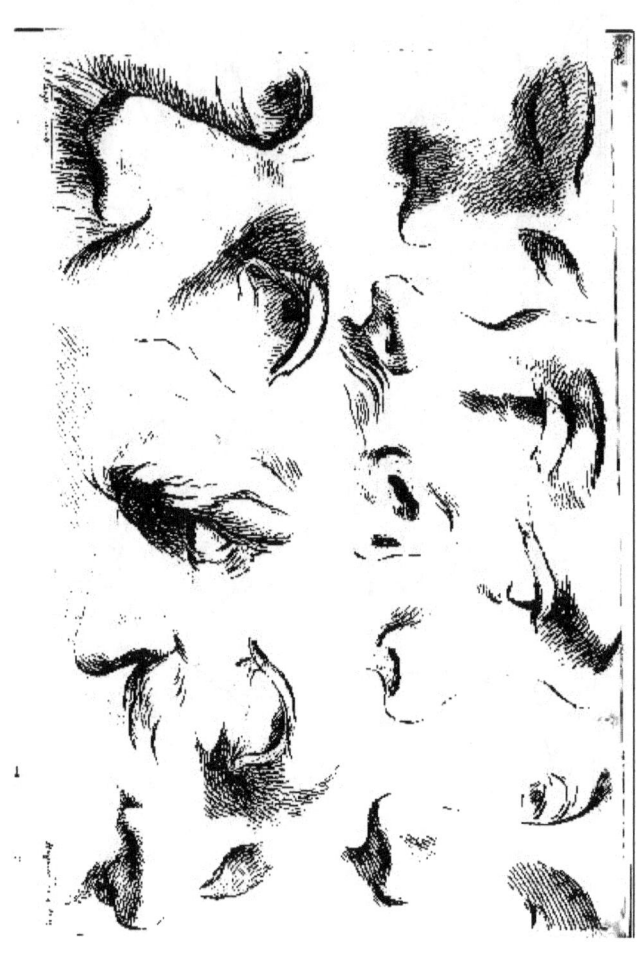

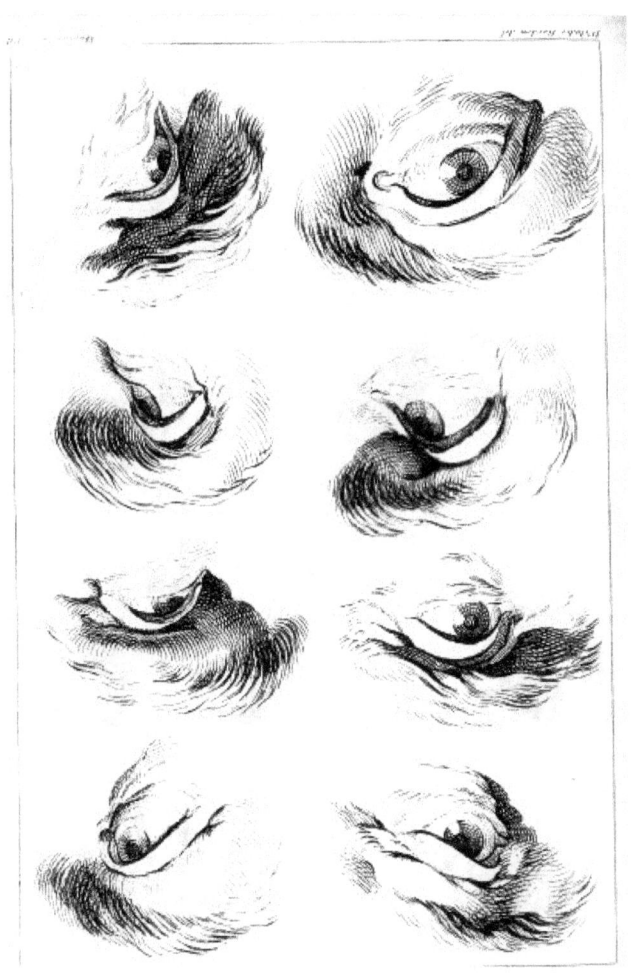

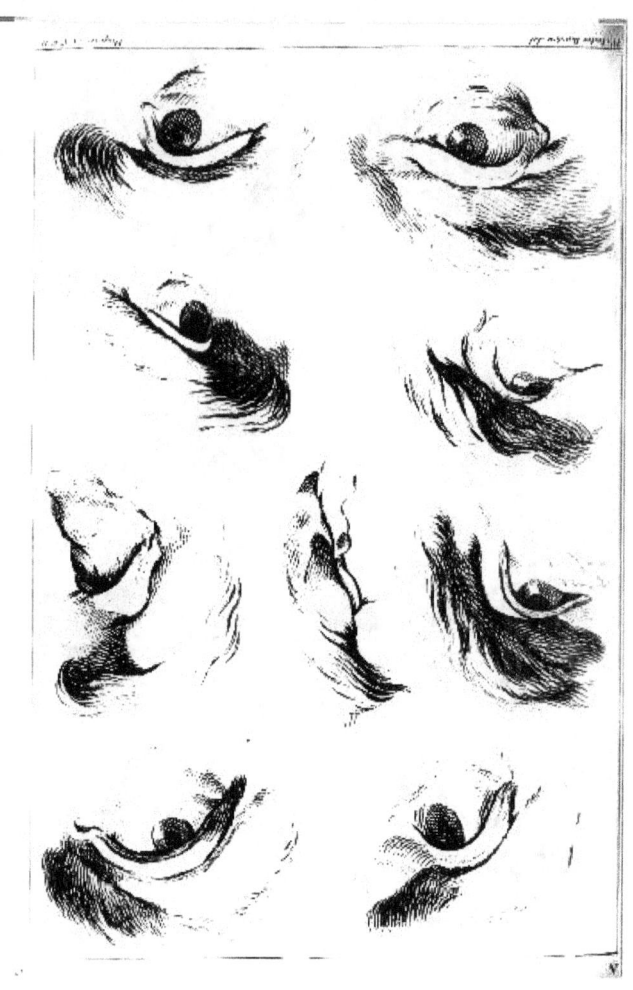

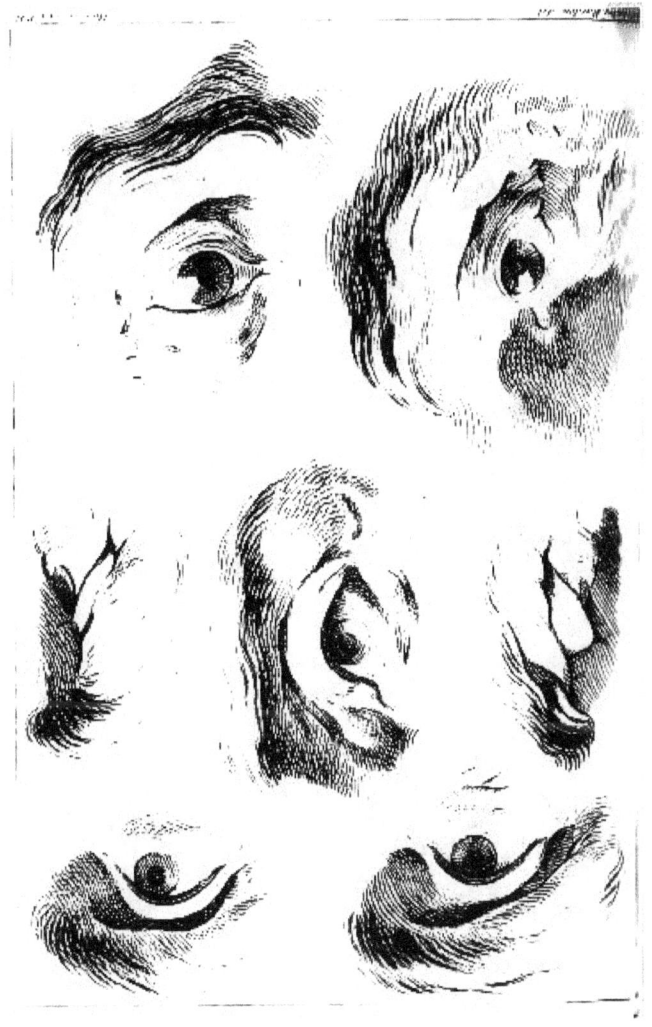

171

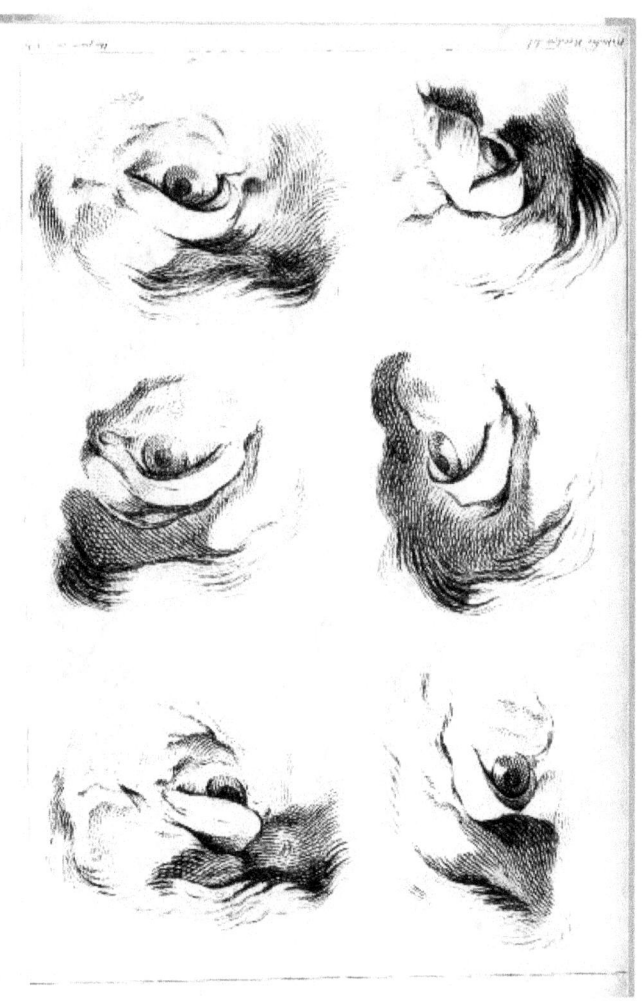

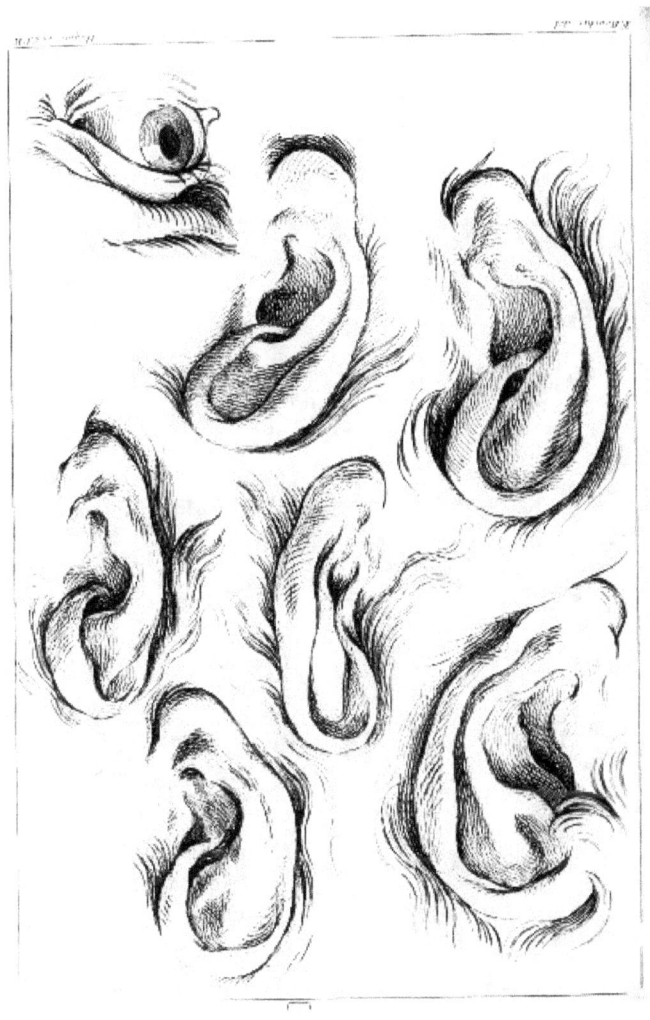

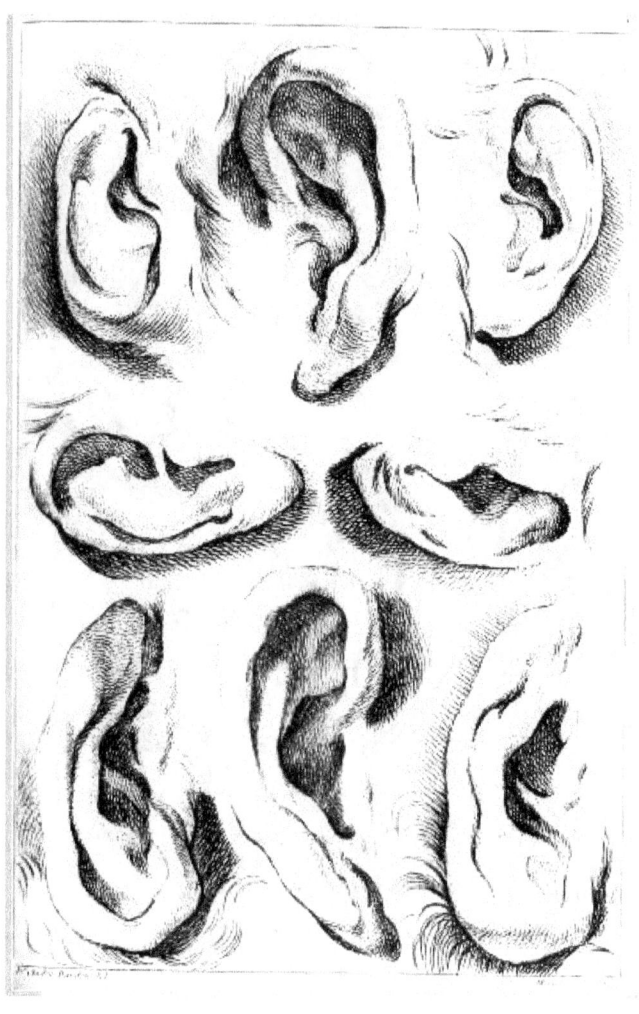

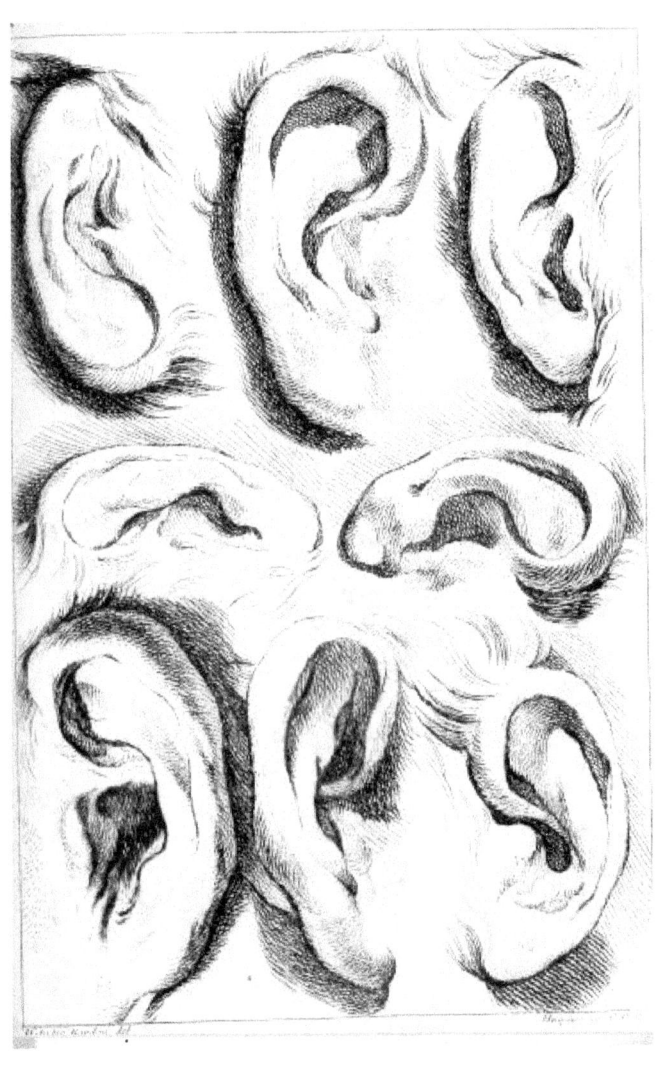

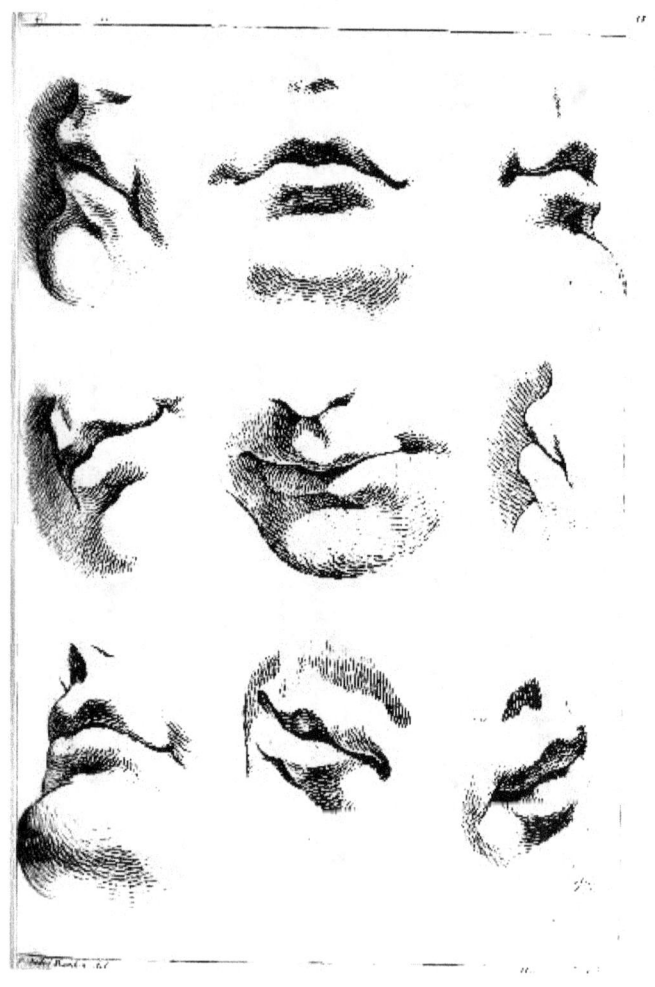

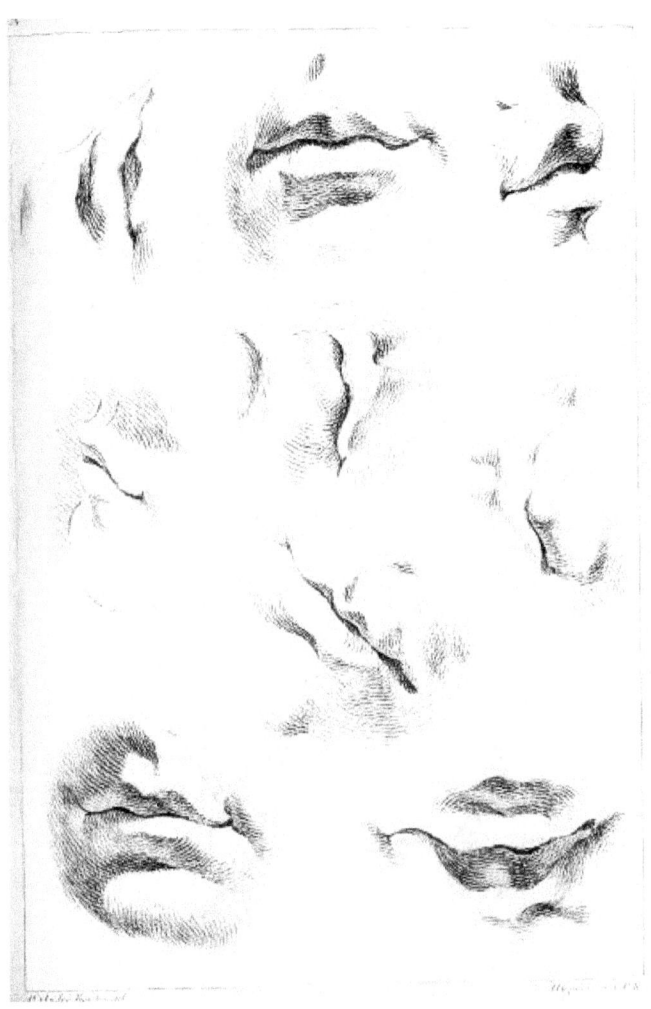

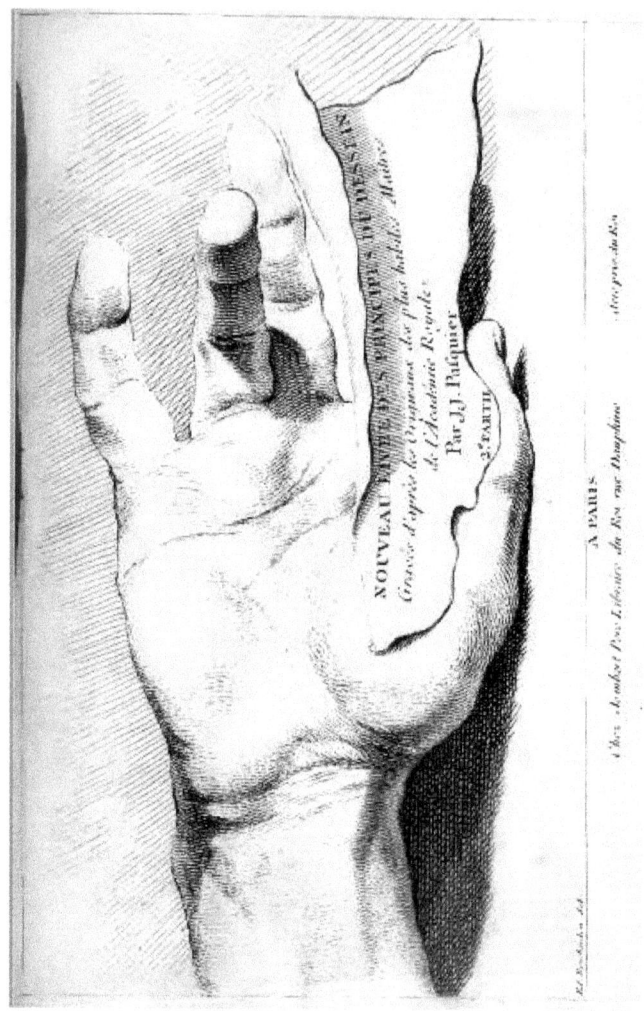

NOUVEAU PRINCIPES DE DESSIN

Gravés d'après les Originaux des plus habiles Maîtres
de l'Académie Royale.

Par J.J. Palquier.

2ᵉ PARTIE.

A PARIS

Chez Audibert Picol. Libraire du Roi rue Dauphine   Avec prix du Roi

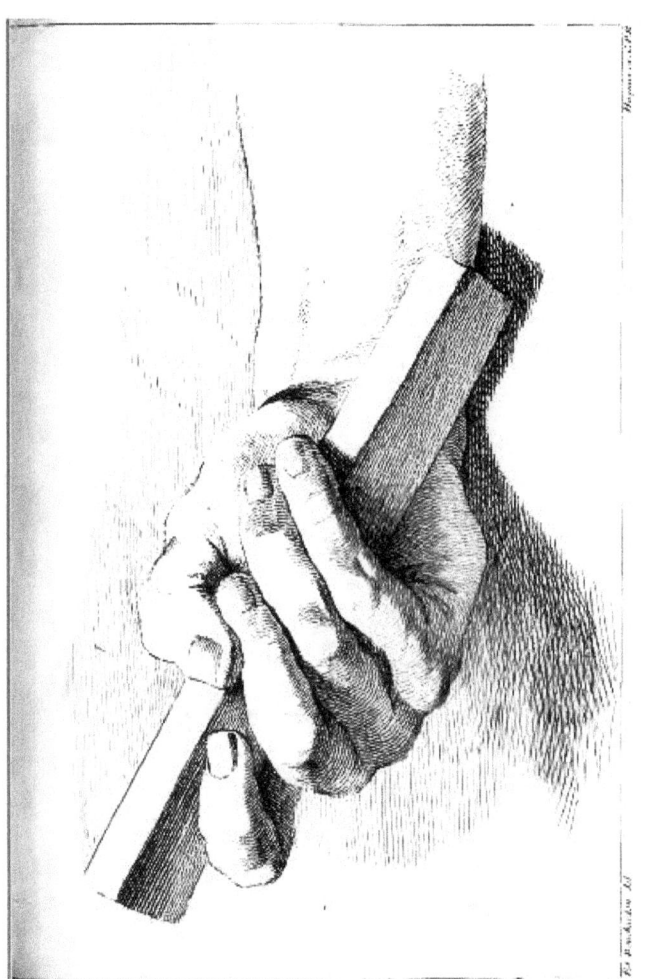

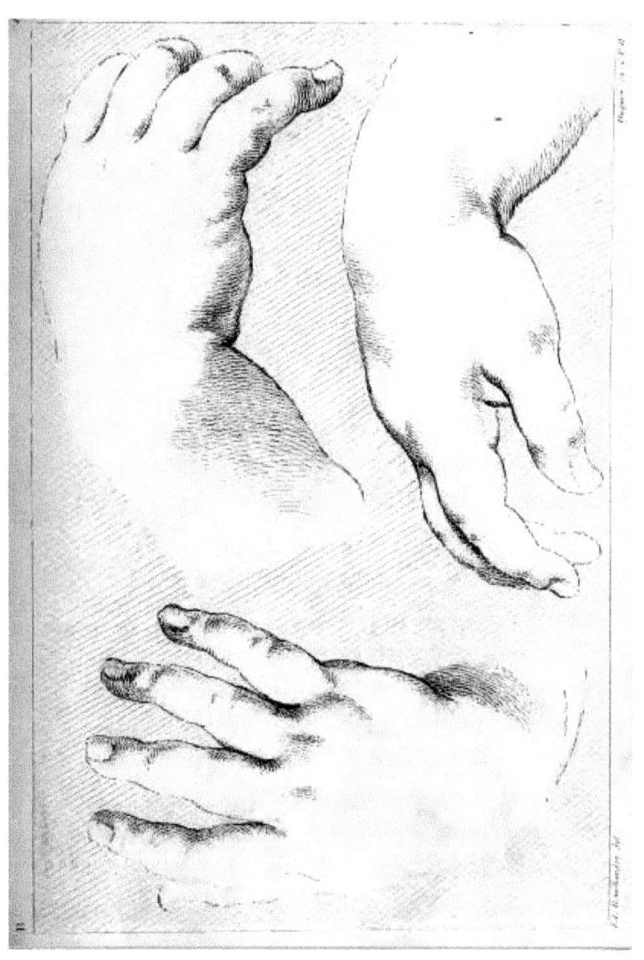

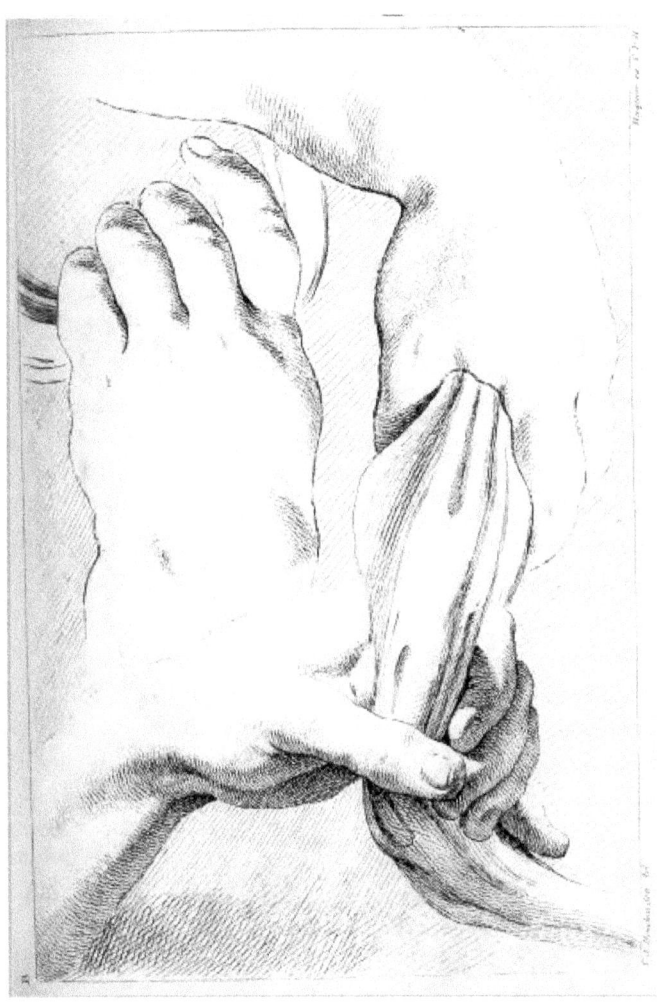

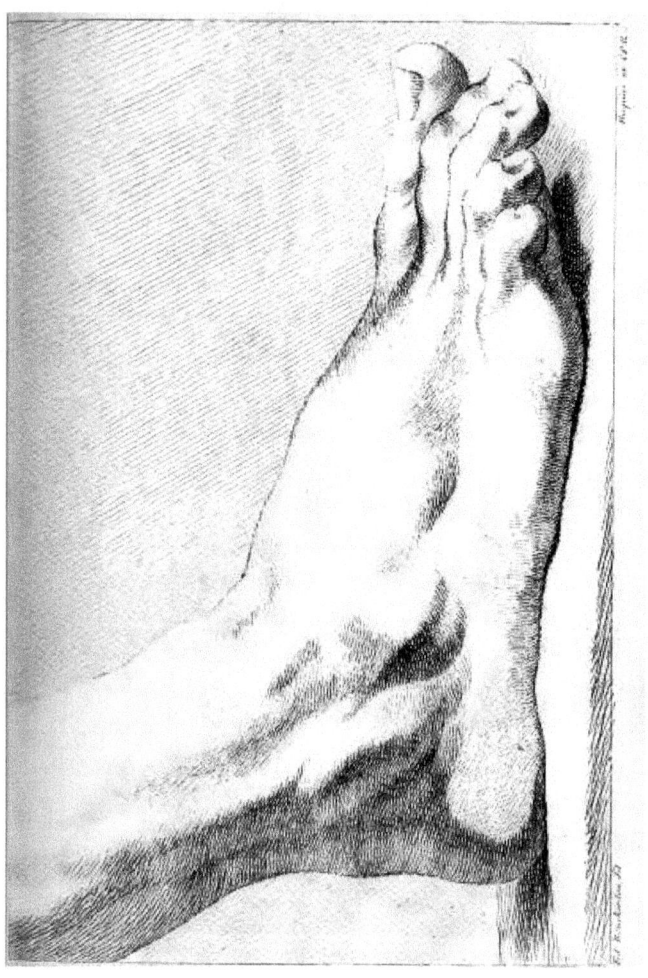

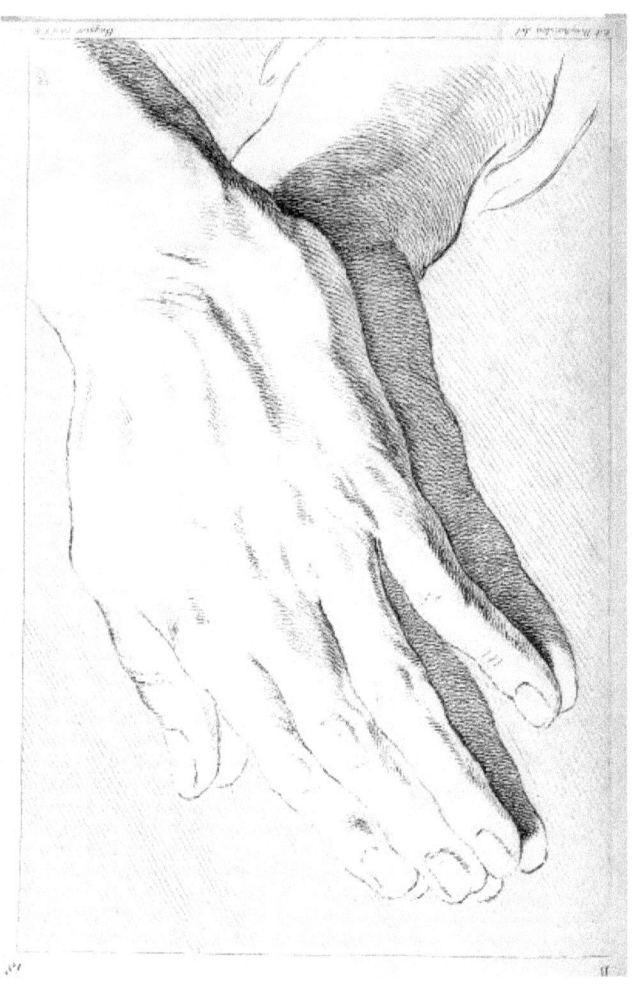

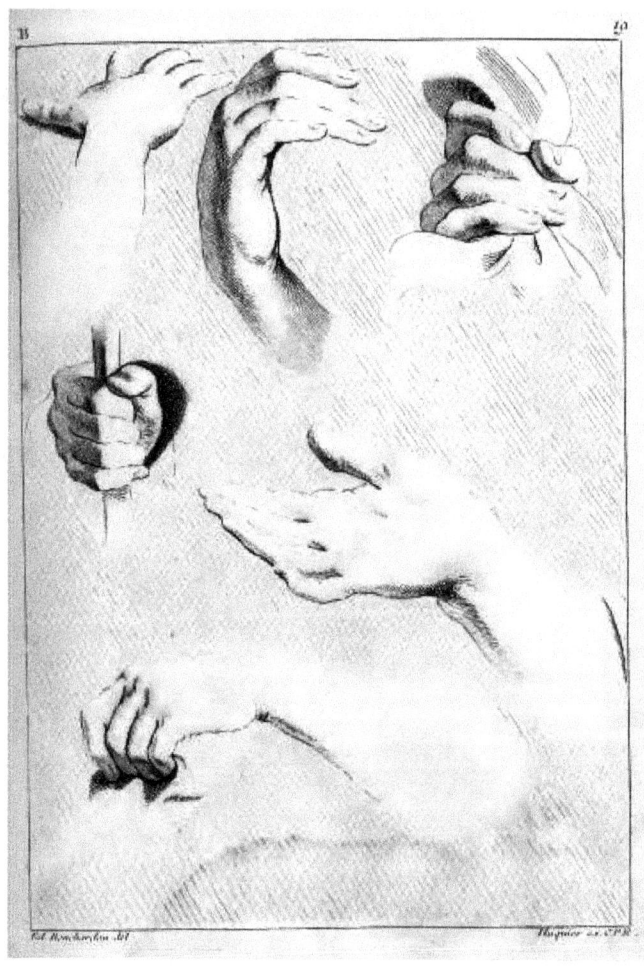

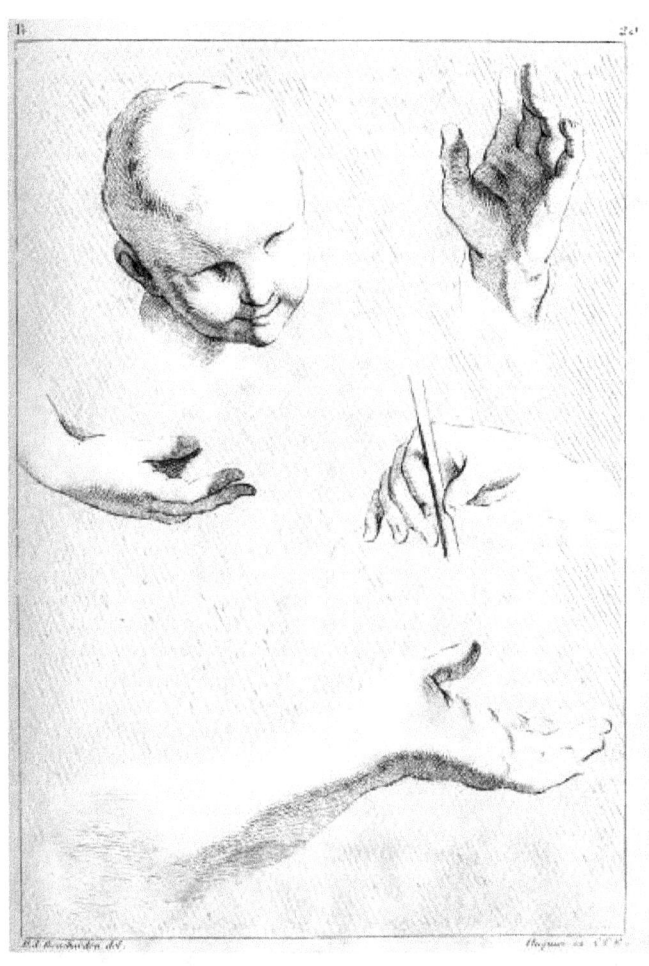

B. J. Bouchardon del. Daguar sc. SCB

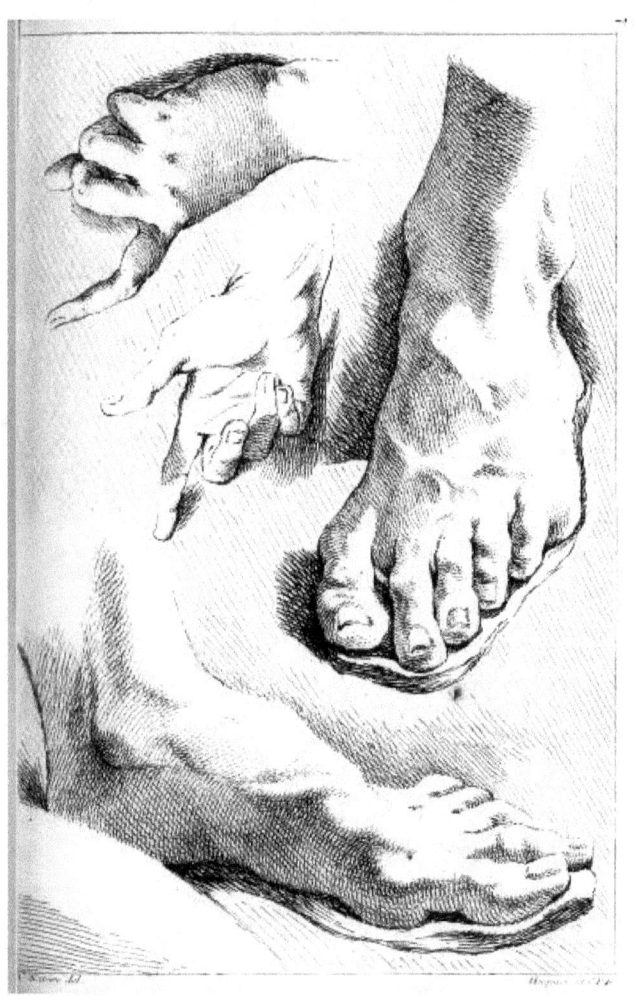

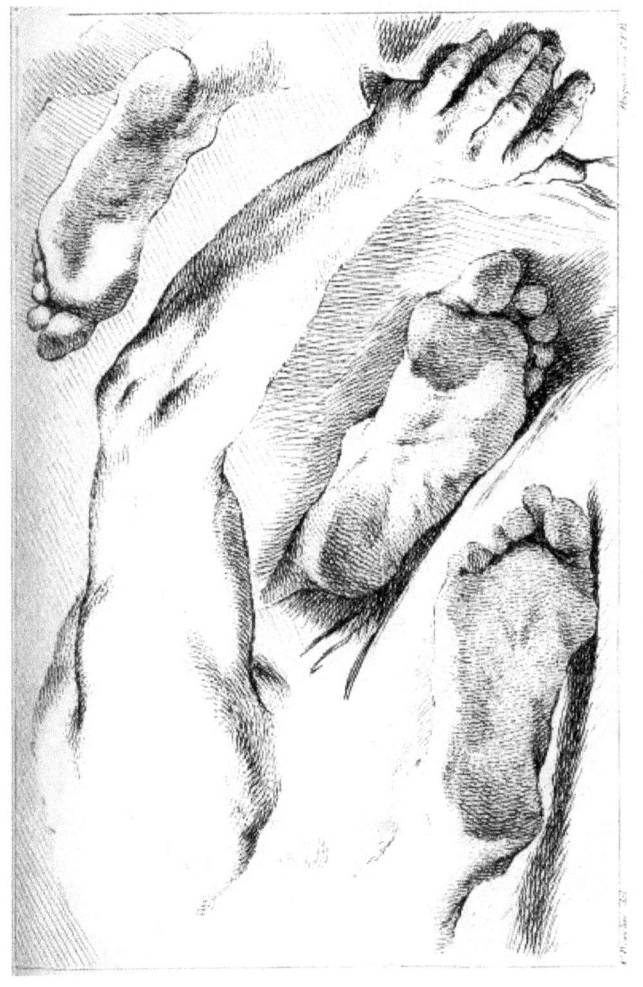

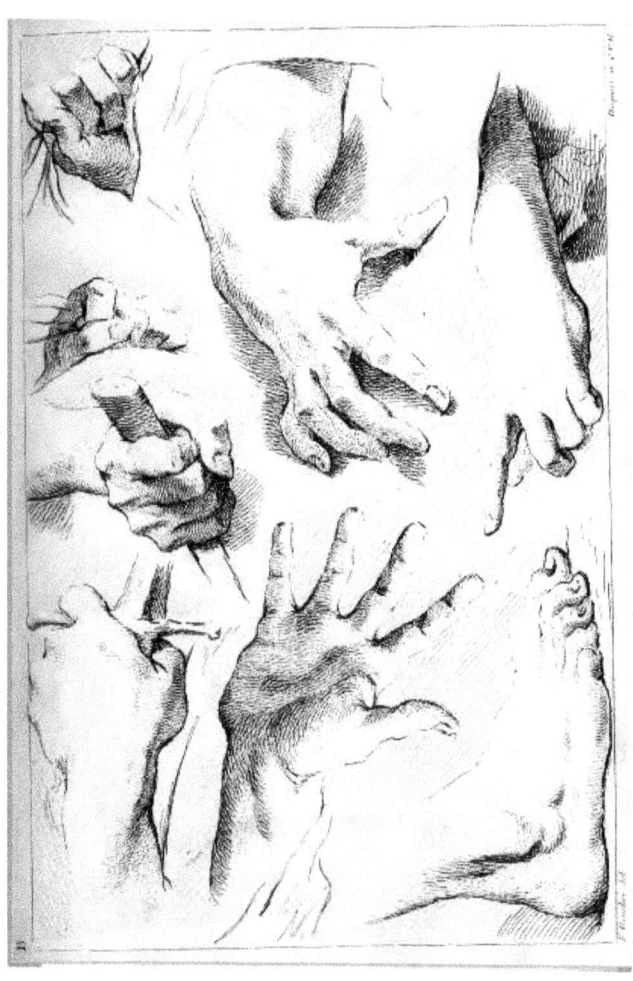

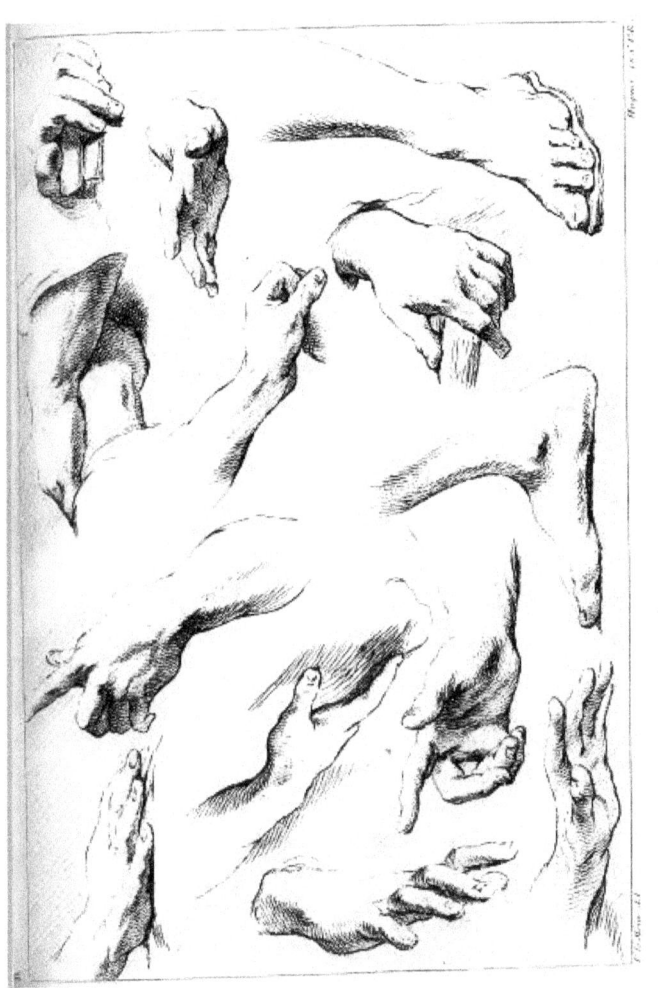

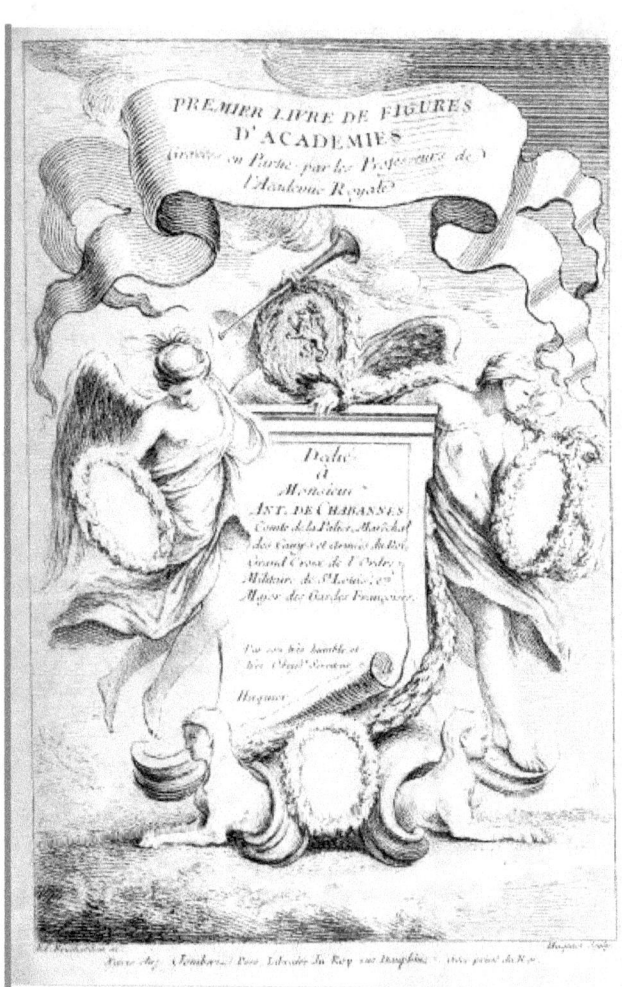

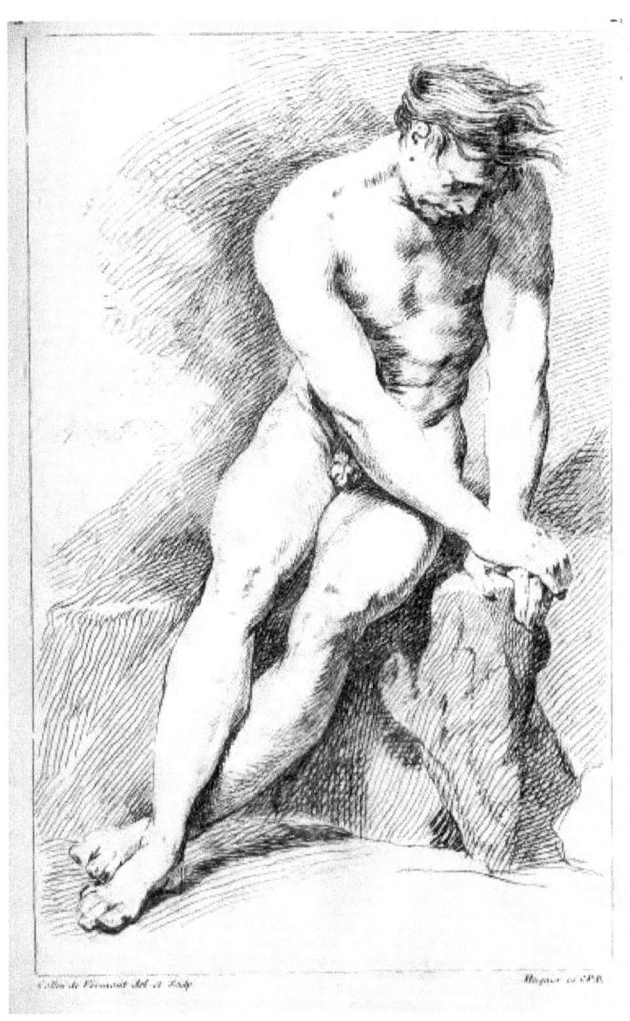

Collin de Vermont del. et Sculp.   Magnus ex CPR.

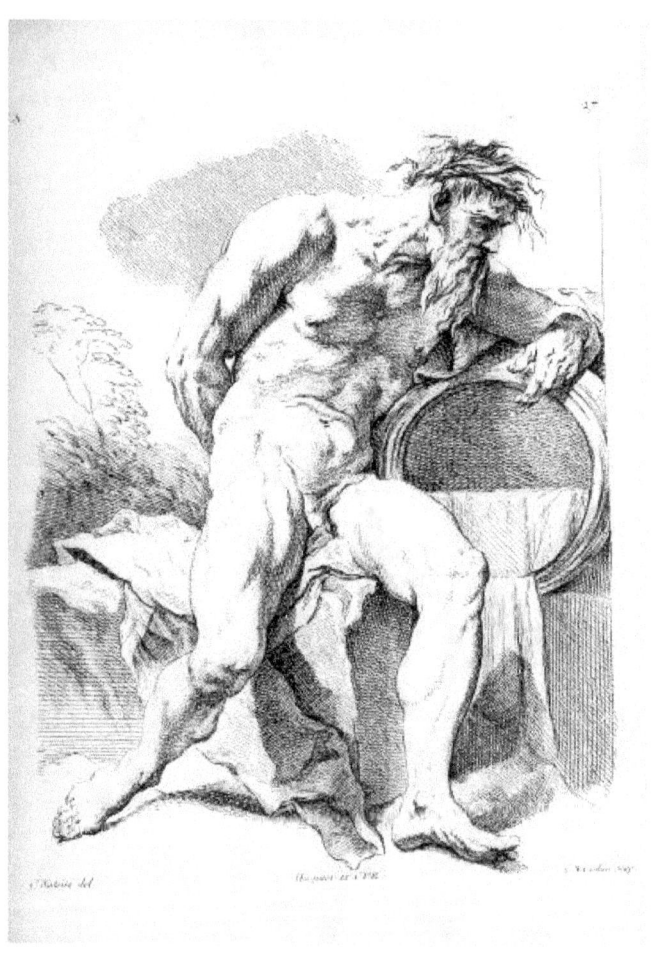

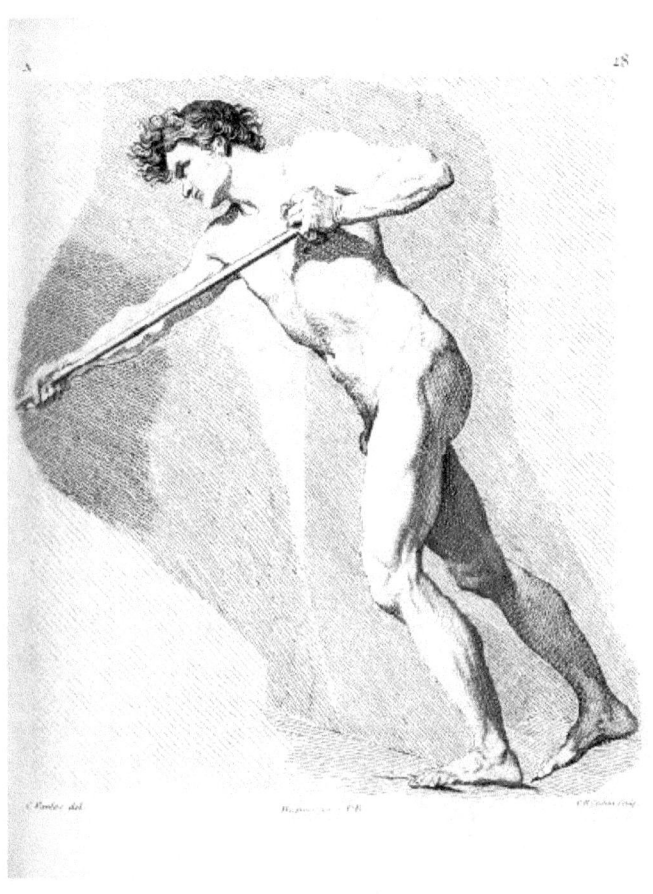

C. Parrier del.

Bajme... C.E.

C.H. Joulain 1809

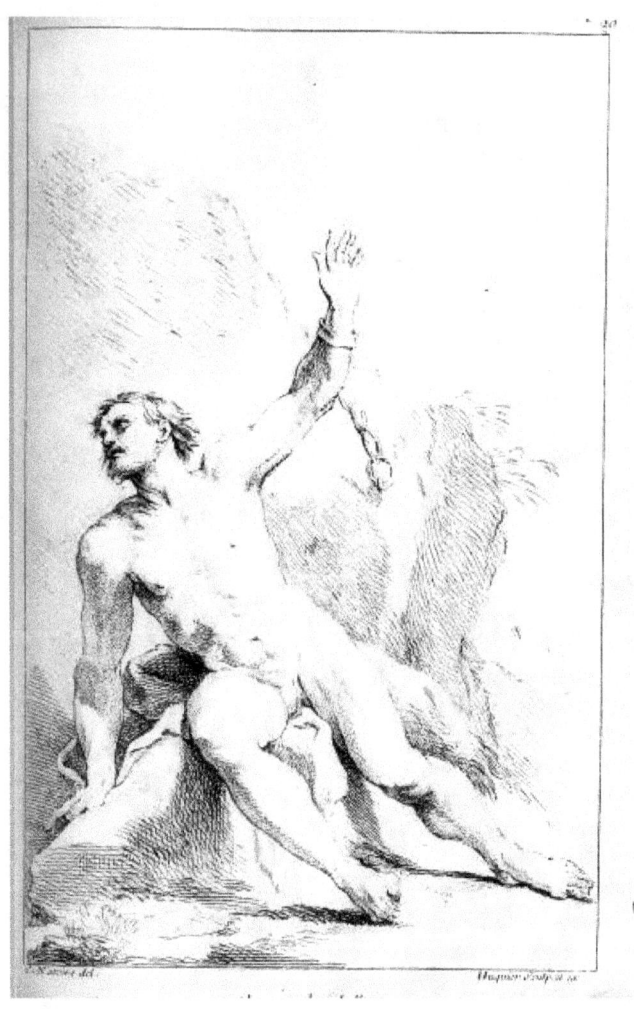

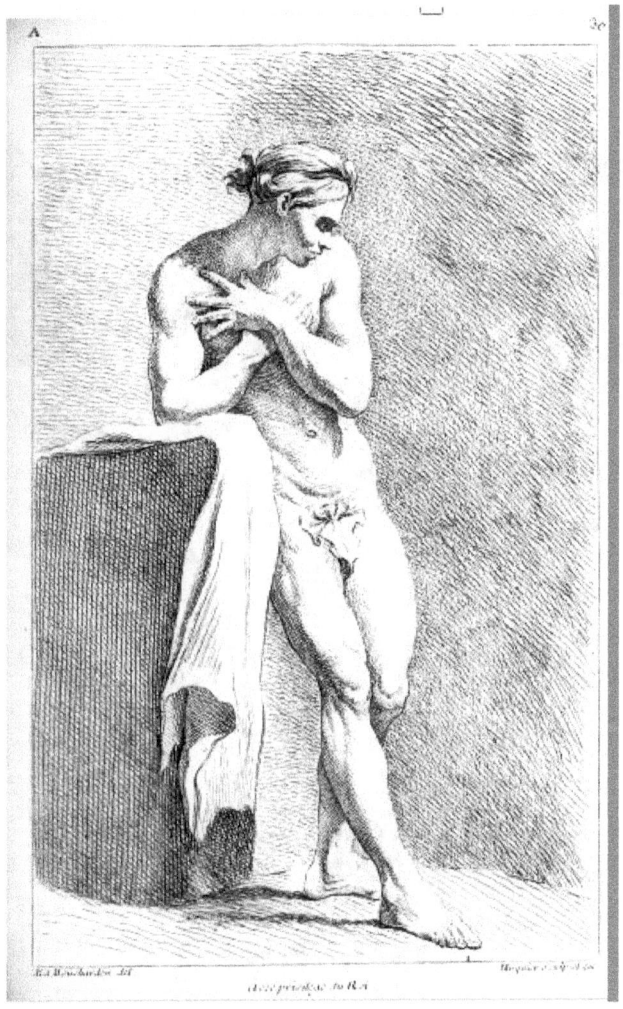

dessiné d'après le Roi

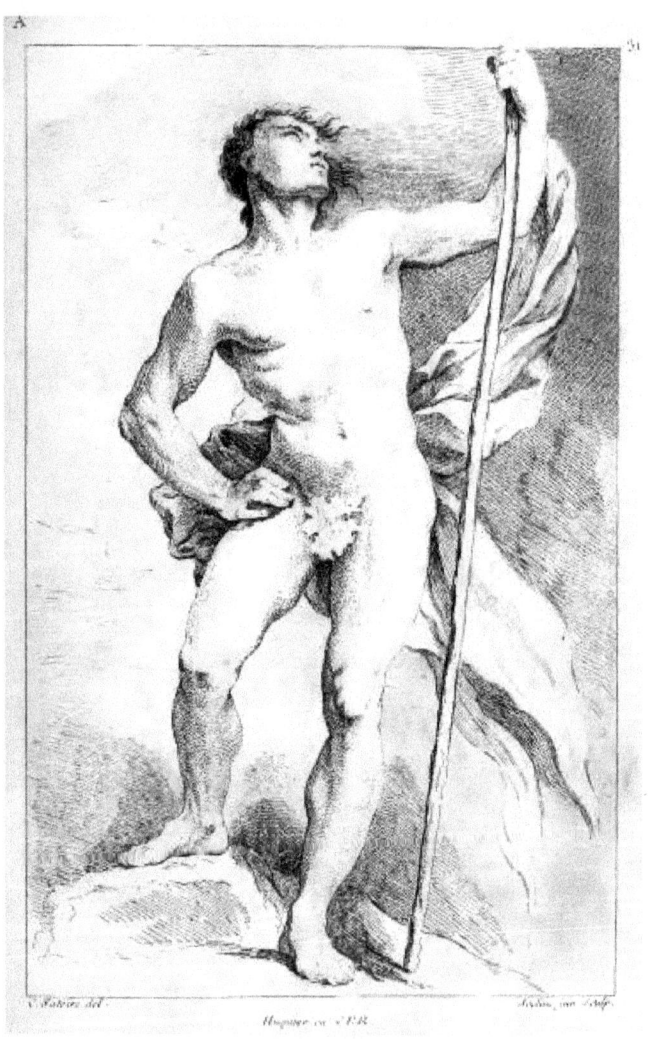

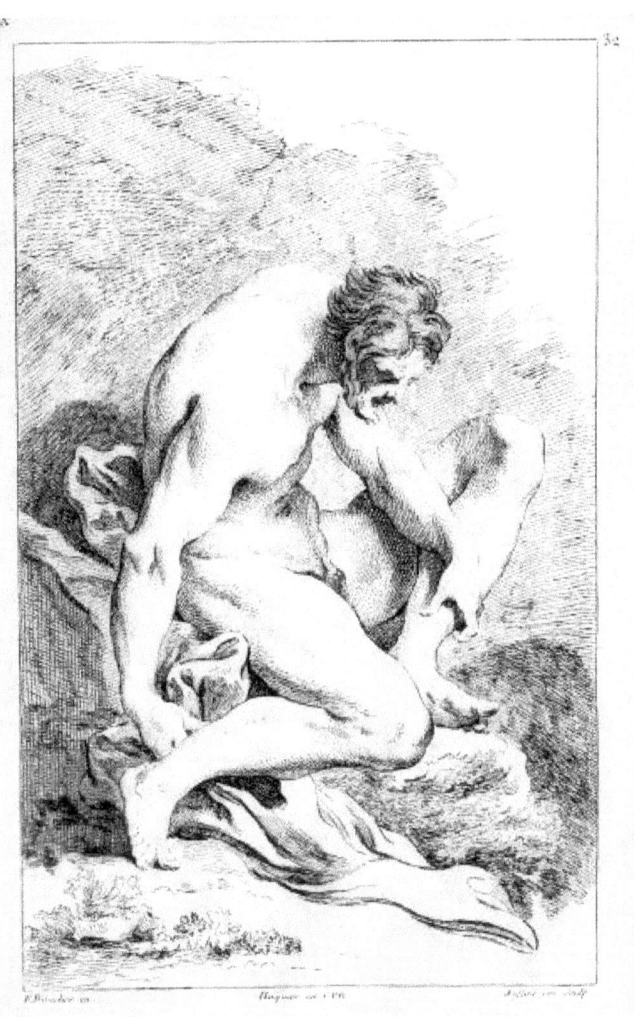

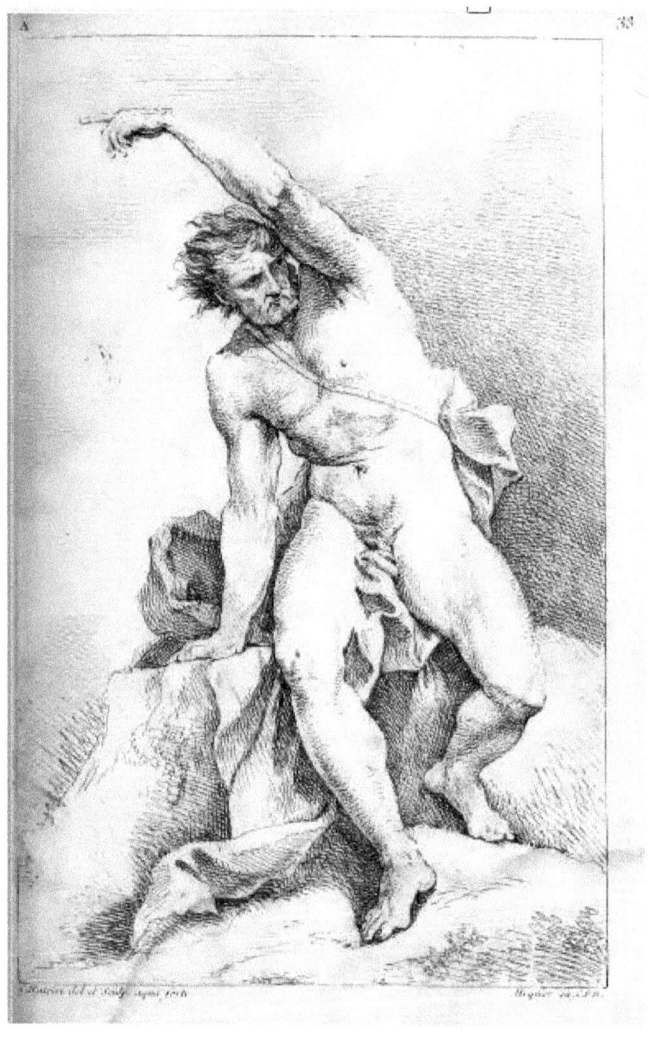

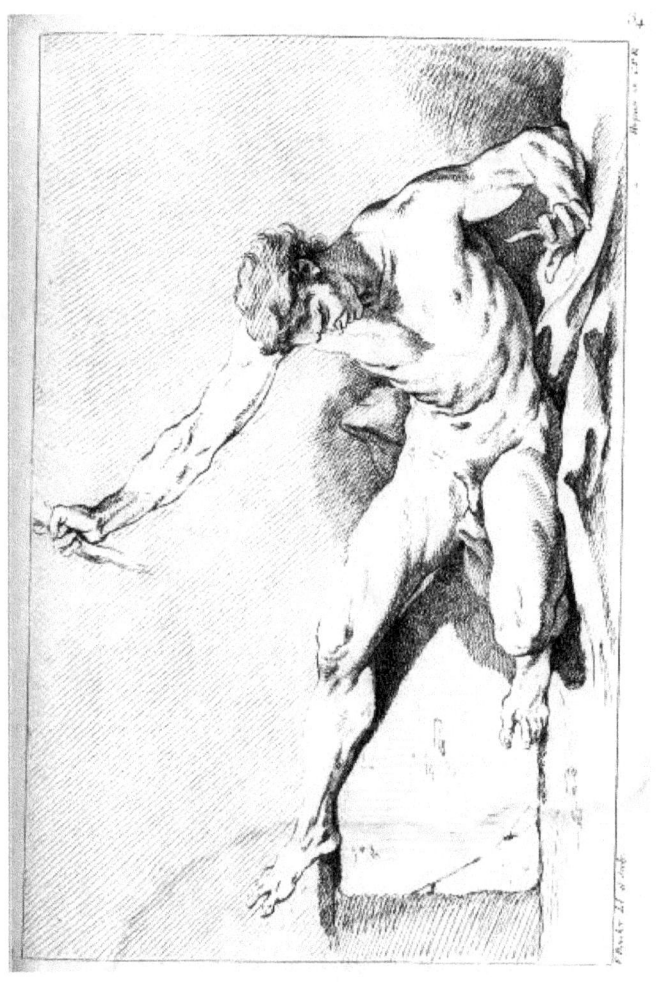

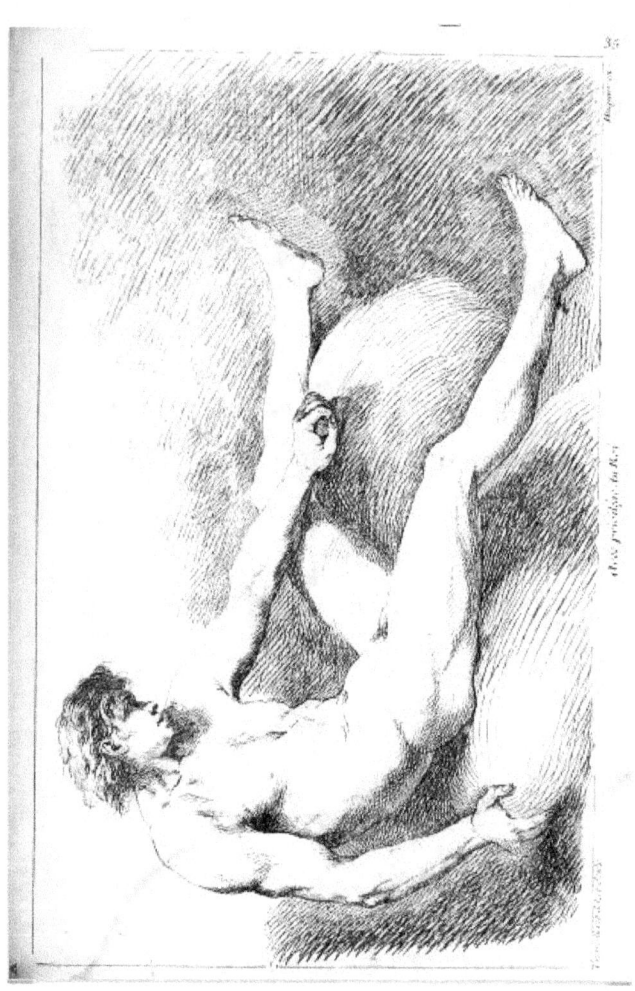

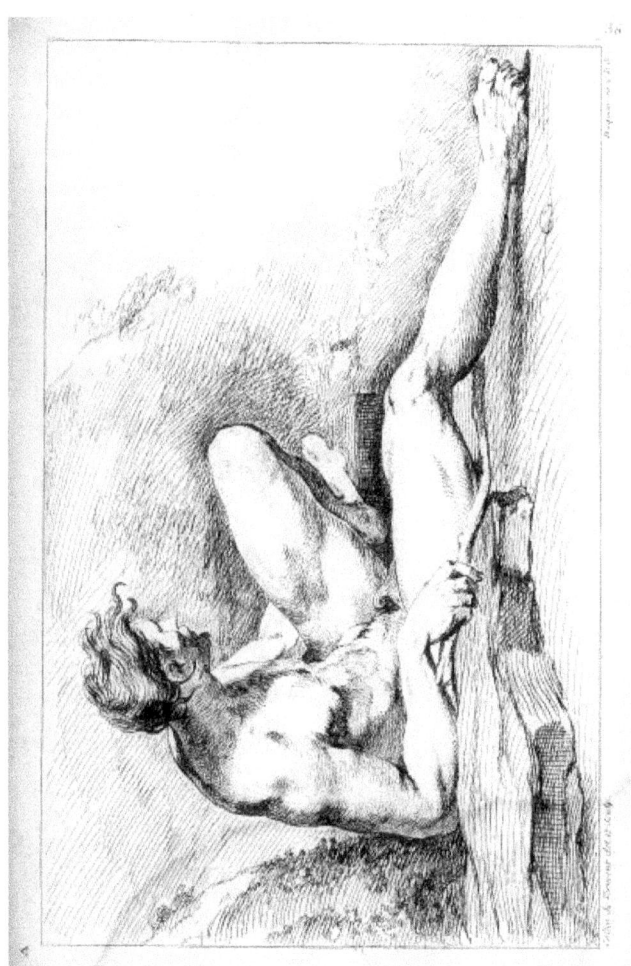

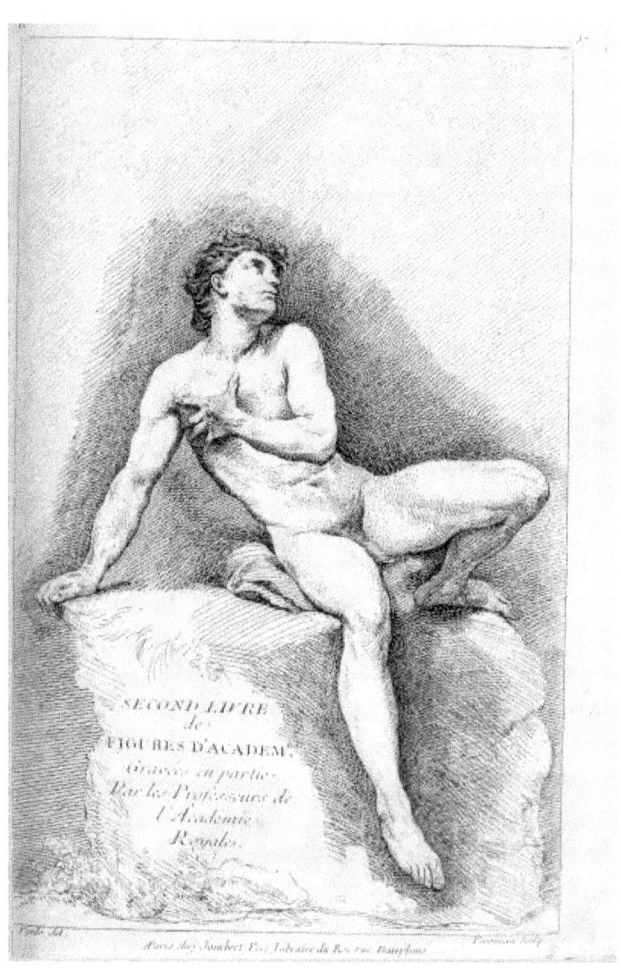

SECOND LIVRE
de
FIGURES D'ACADEM.
Gravées en partie
Par les Professeurs de
l'Académie
Royales.

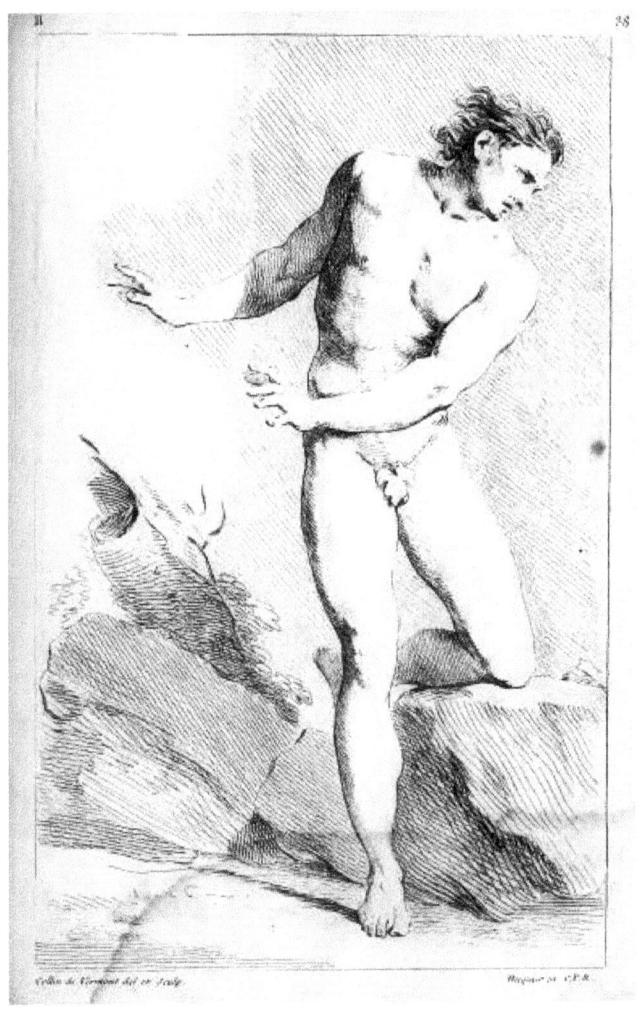

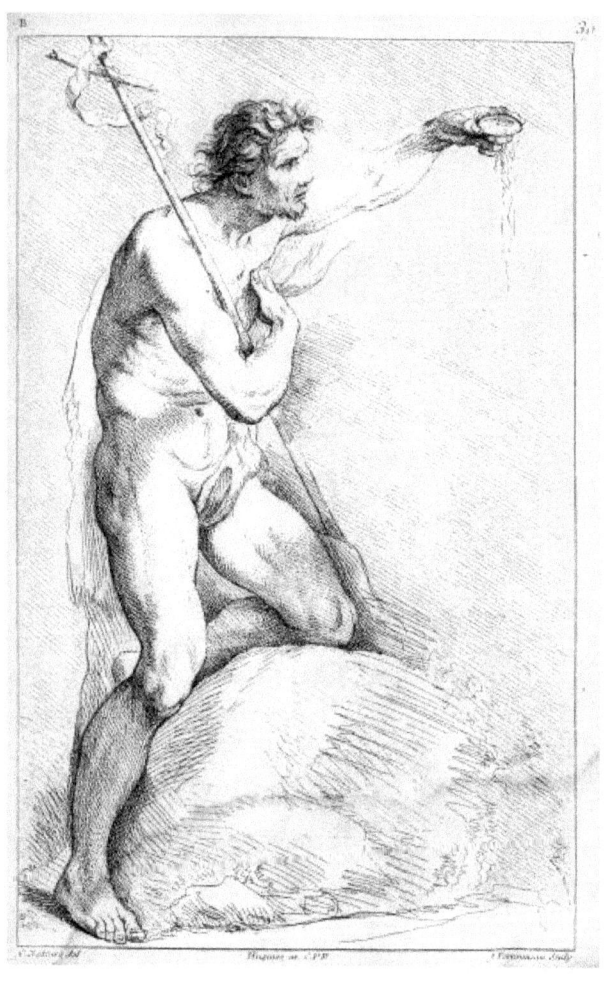

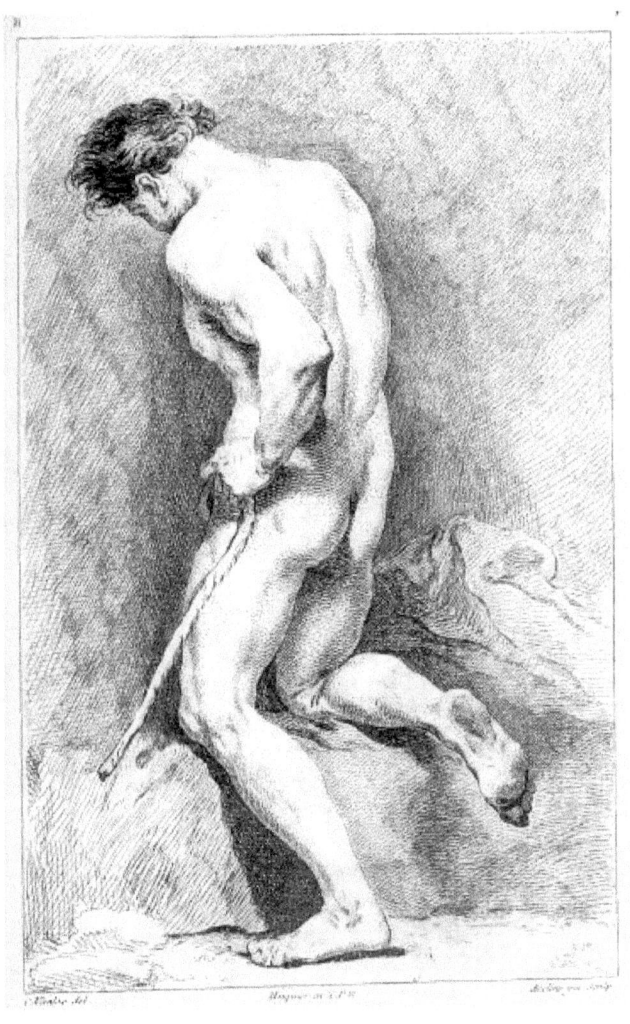

Cochin del.   Huquier ex CPR   Aubry sen. sculp.

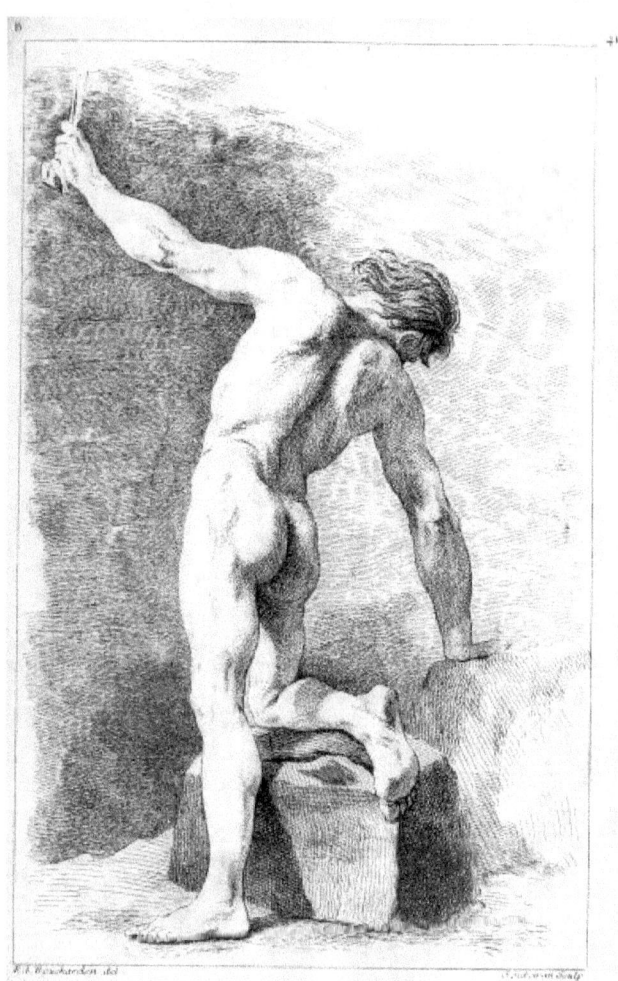

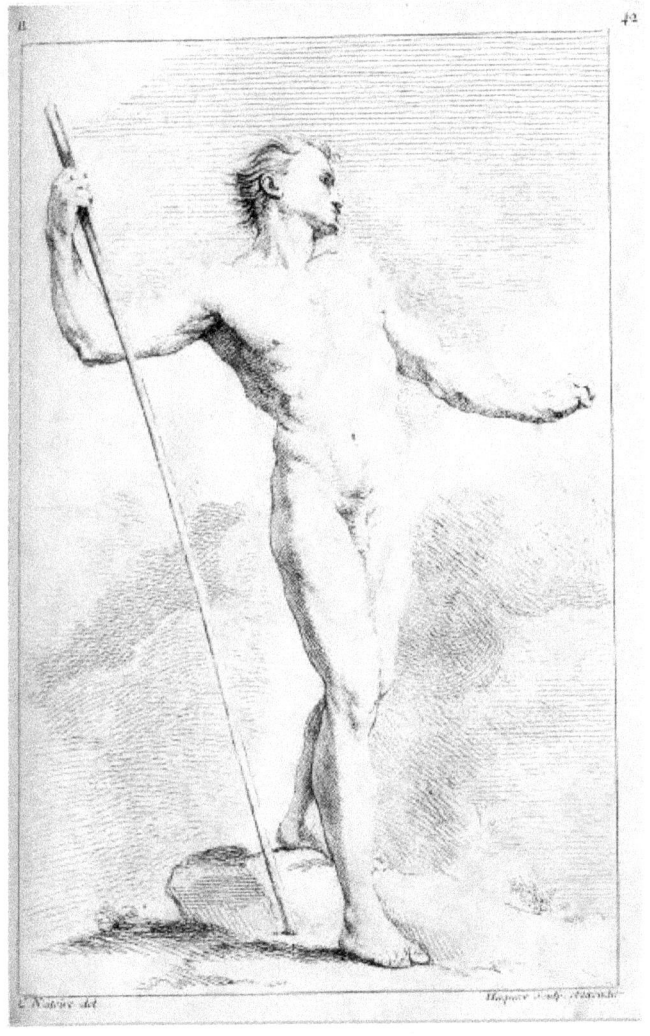

II.

42

C. Natoire del.   Haquier sculp. Alexandri

207

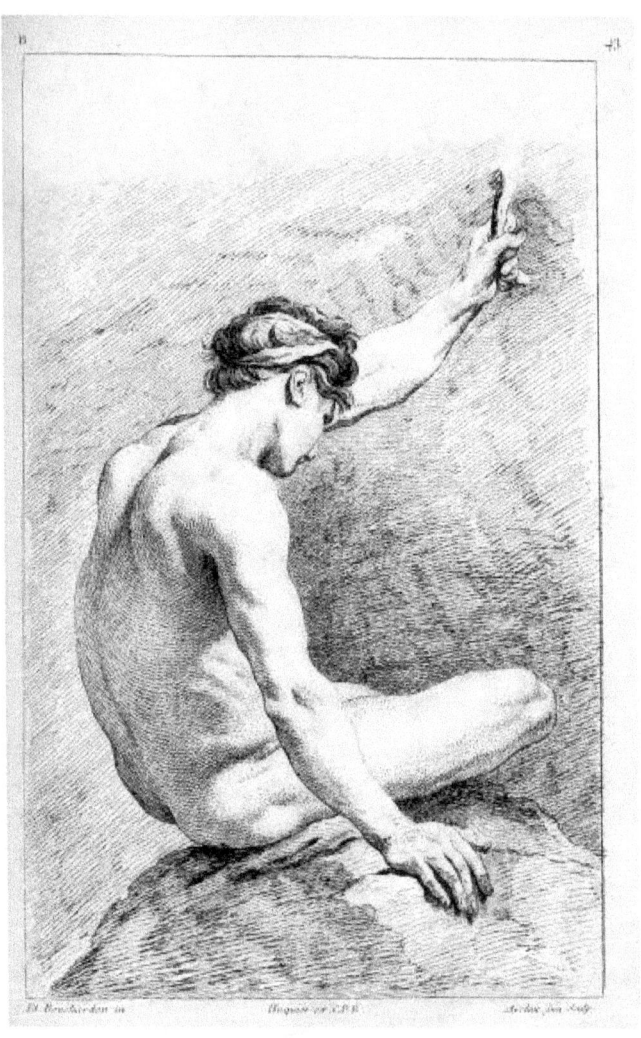

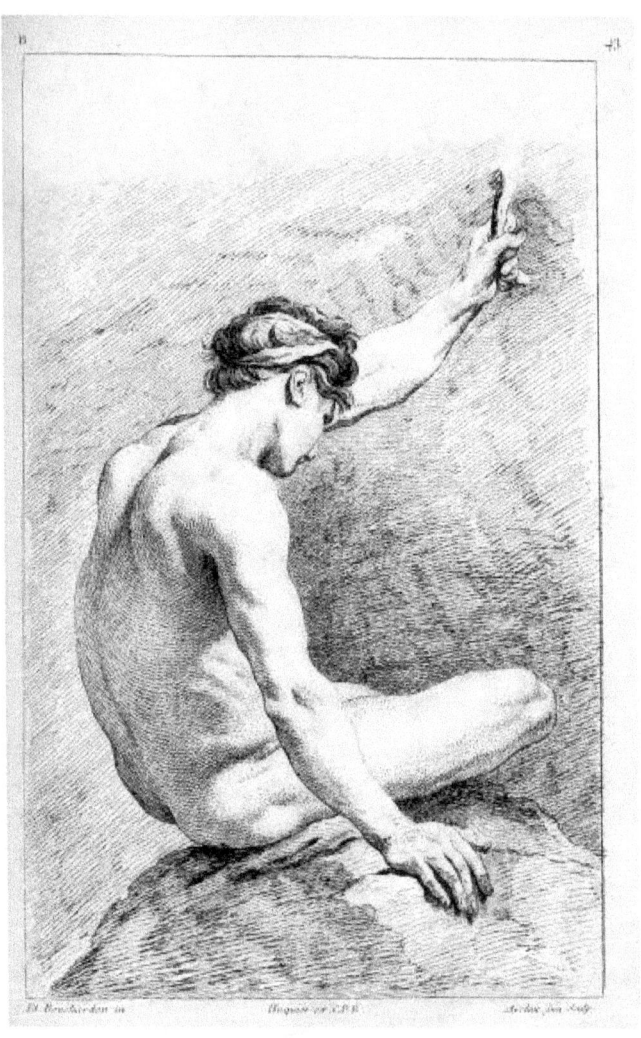

Et. Bouchardon in.   Chaquin ex C.P.R.   Auclut fou Scul.

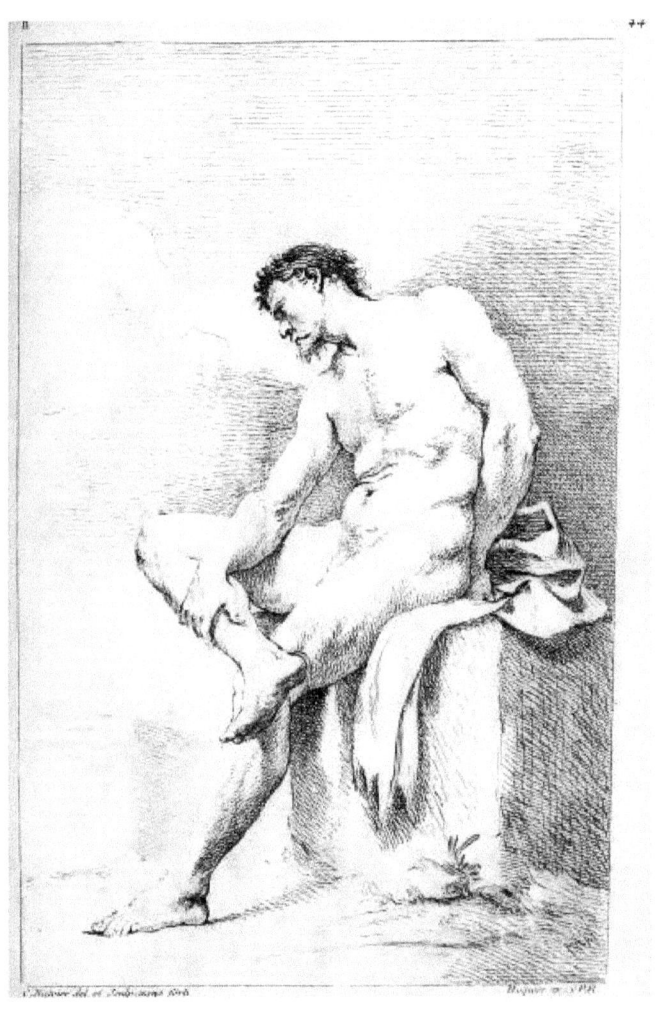

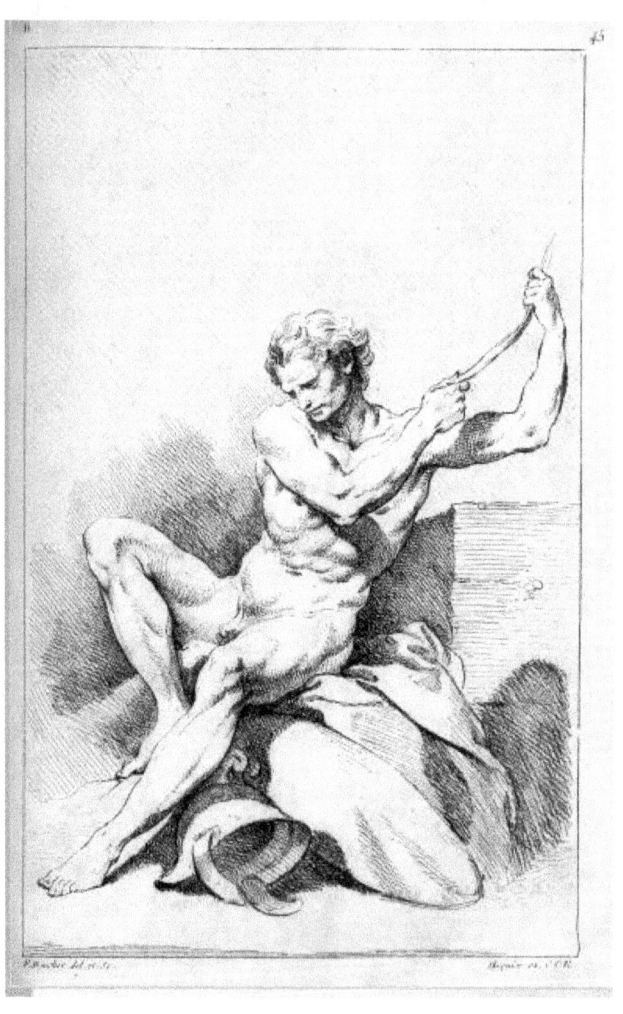

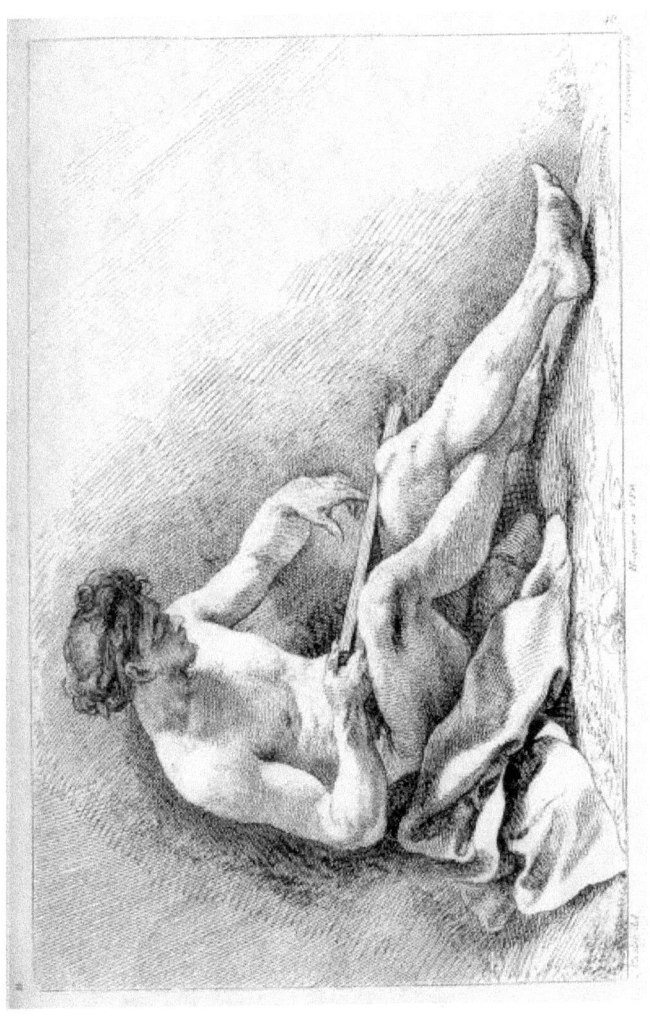

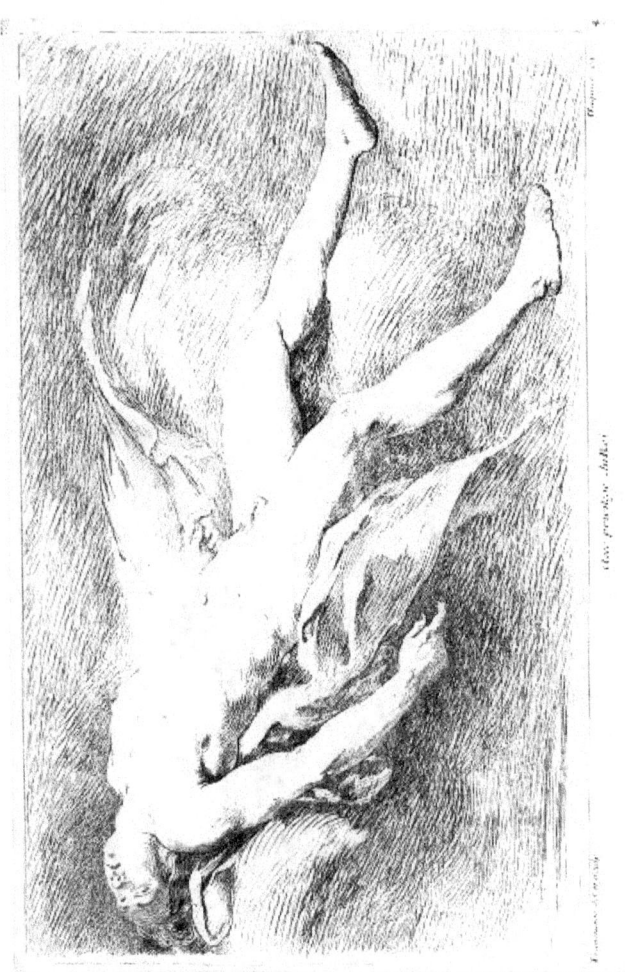

212

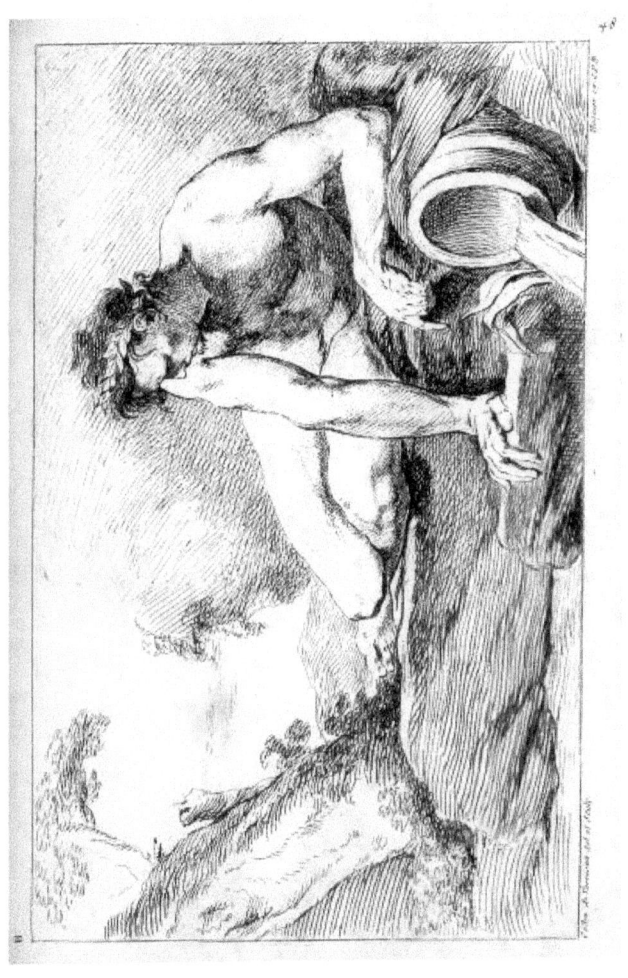

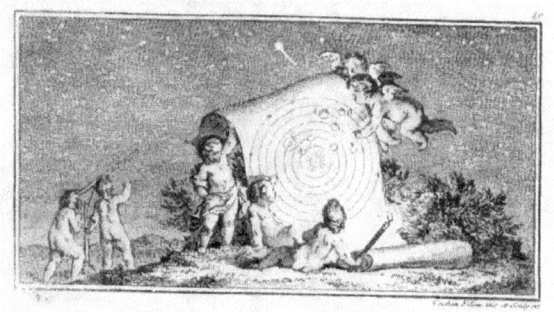

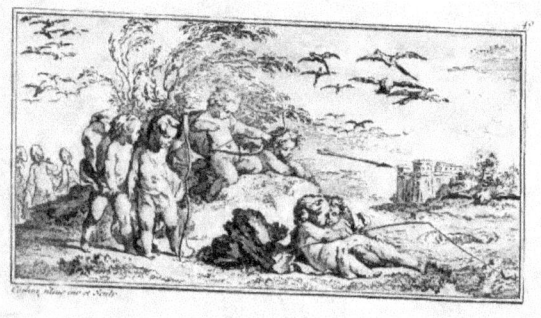

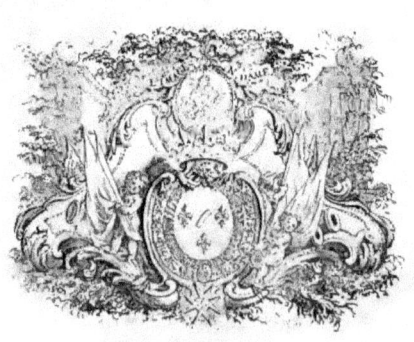

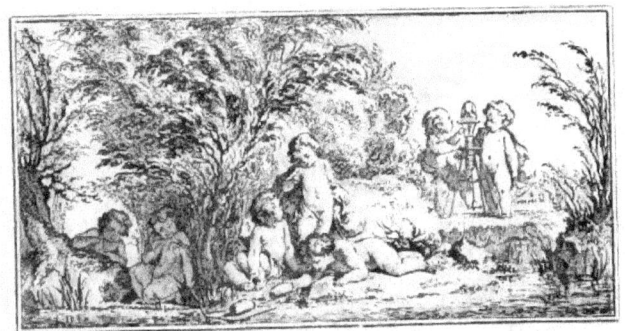

Cochin filius invent Sculp.

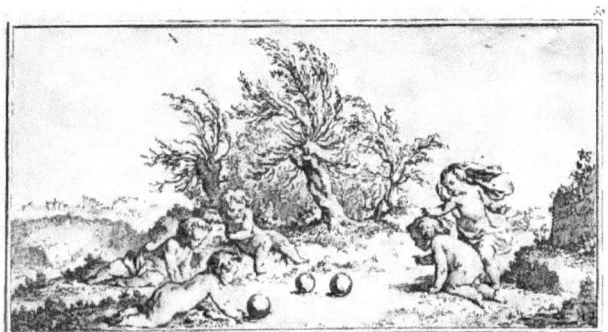

Cochin filius invent Sculp.

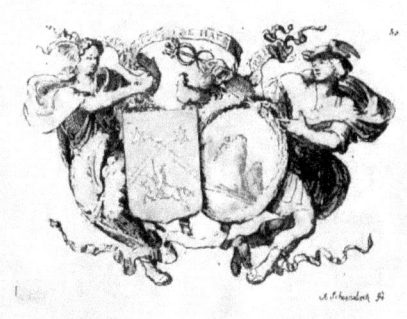

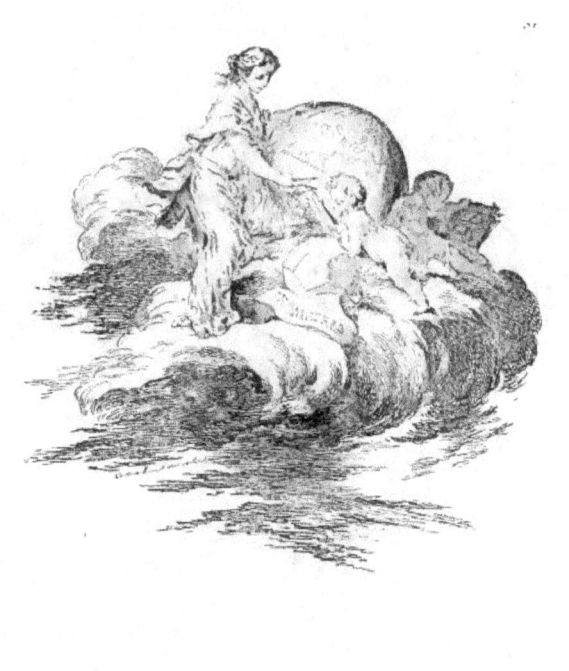

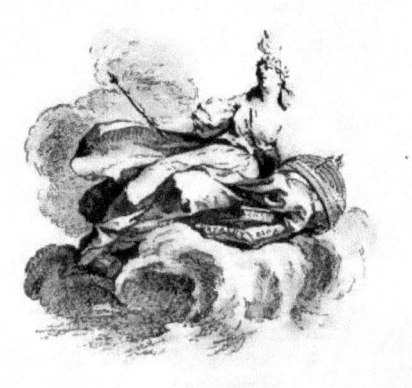

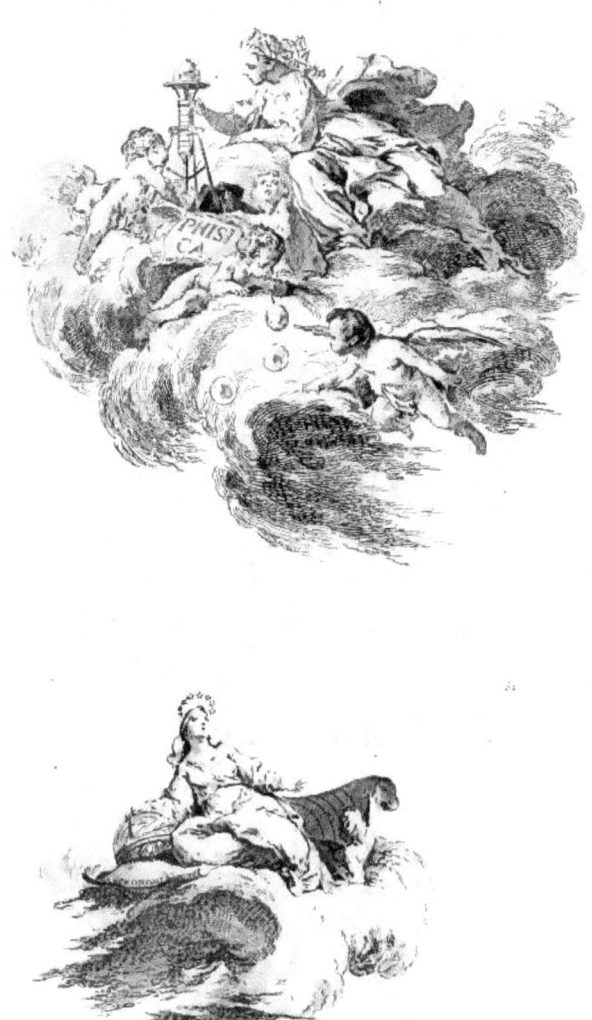

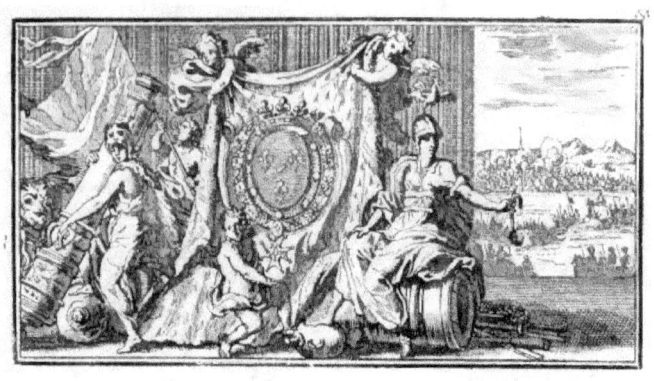

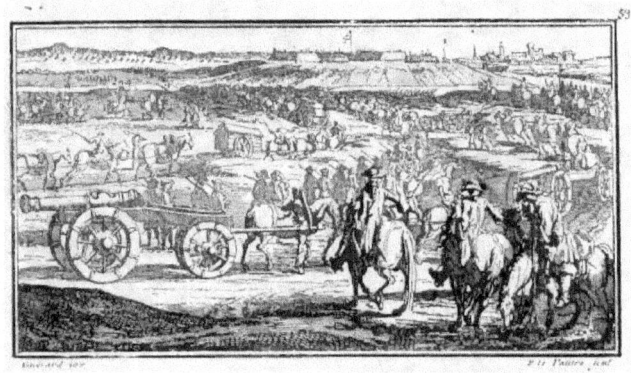

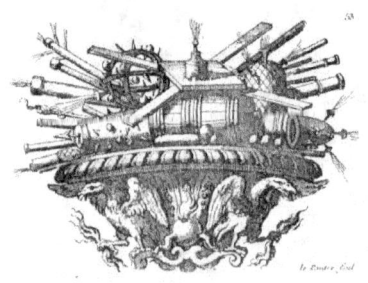

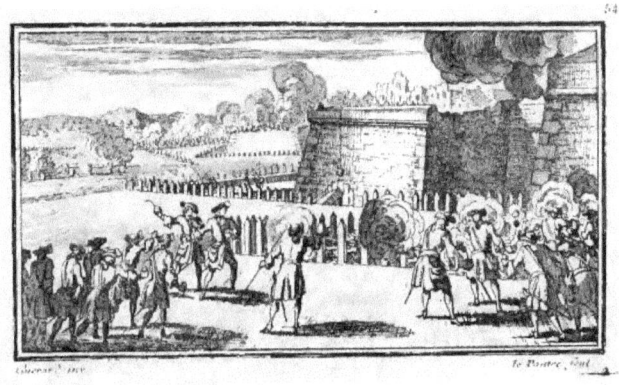

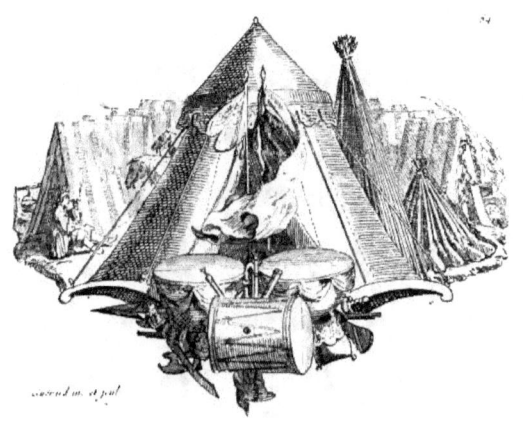

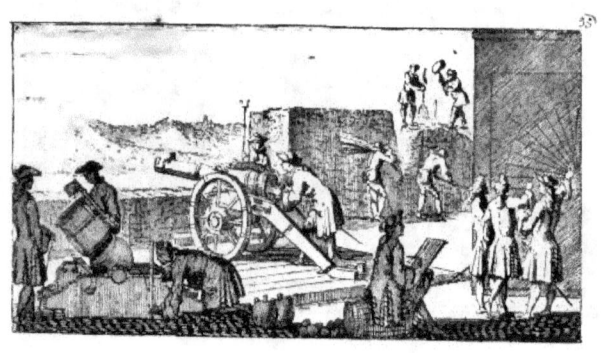

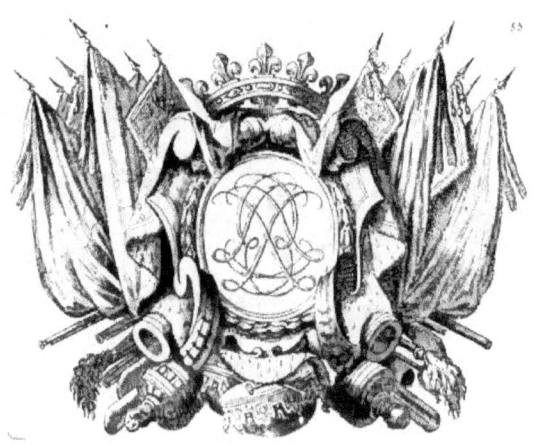

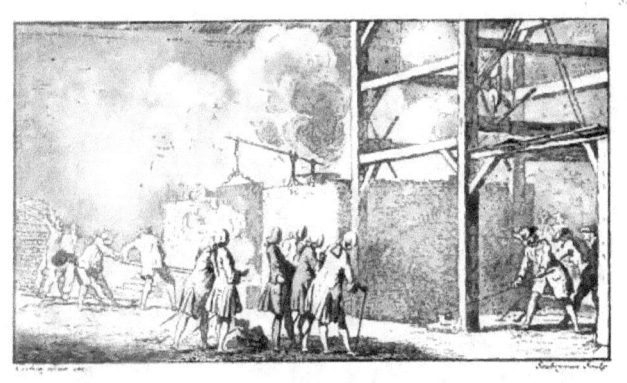

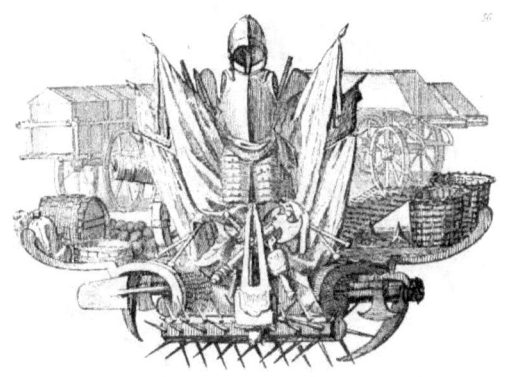

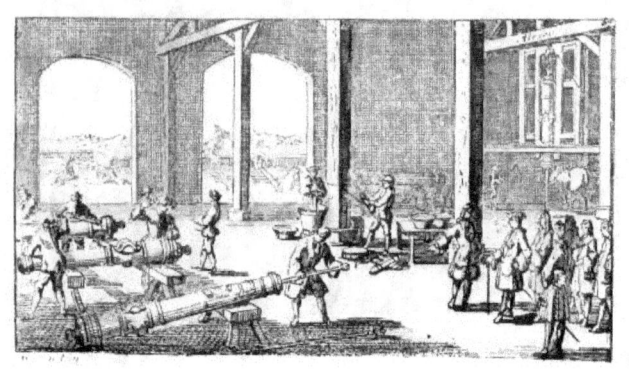

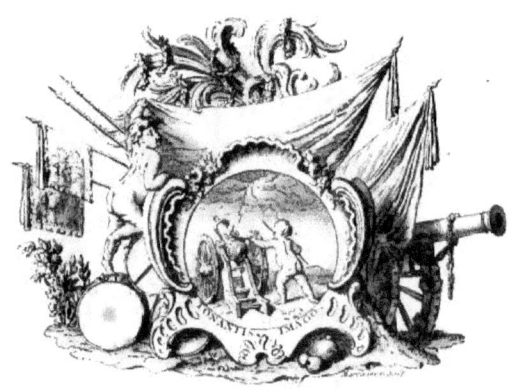

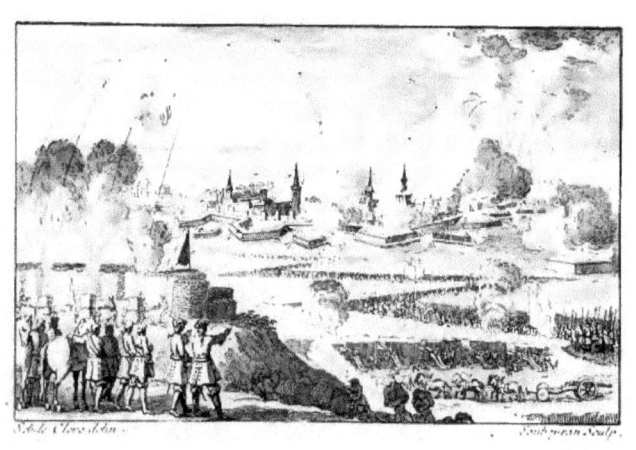

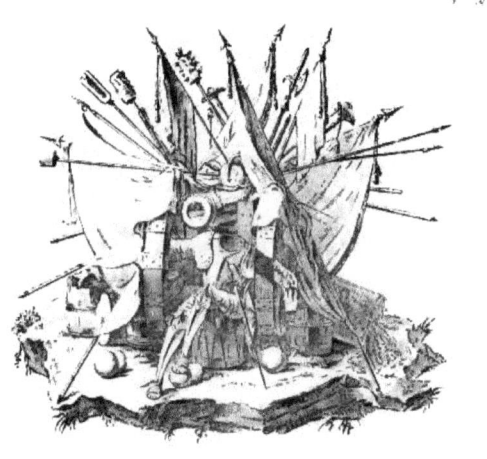

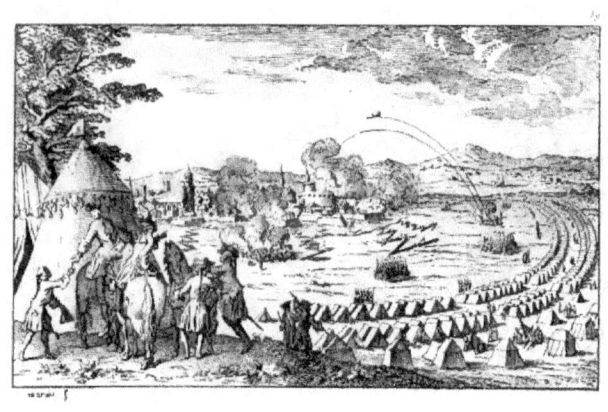

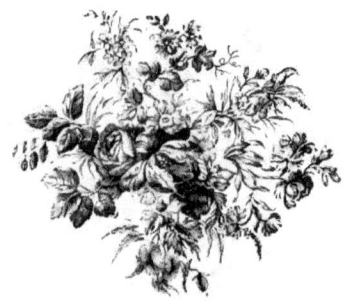

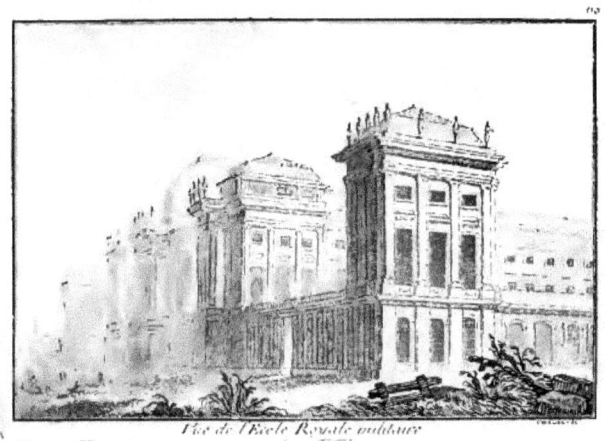

Vue de l'Ecole Royale militaire

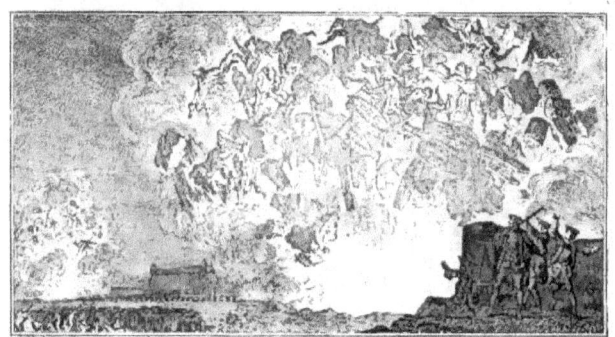

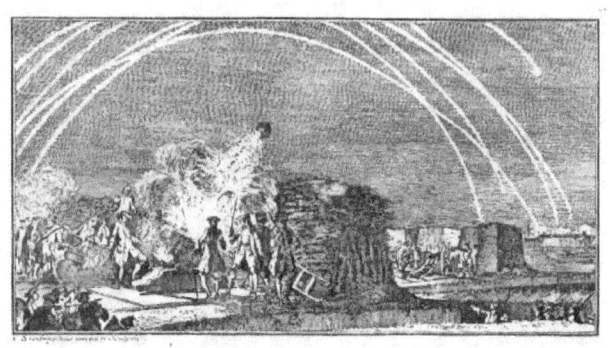

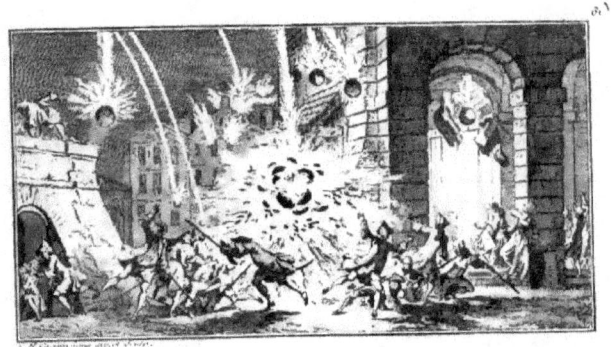

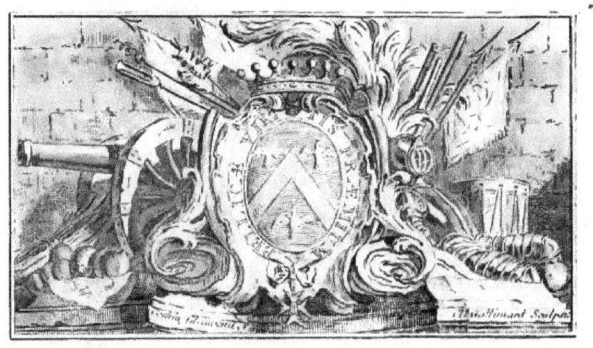

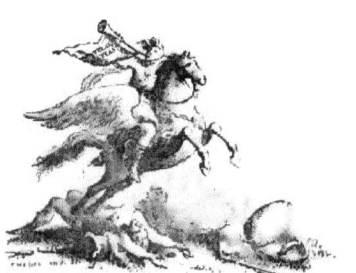

Irruit et qua tela videt densissima tendit
Virg. Æn. l. 9.

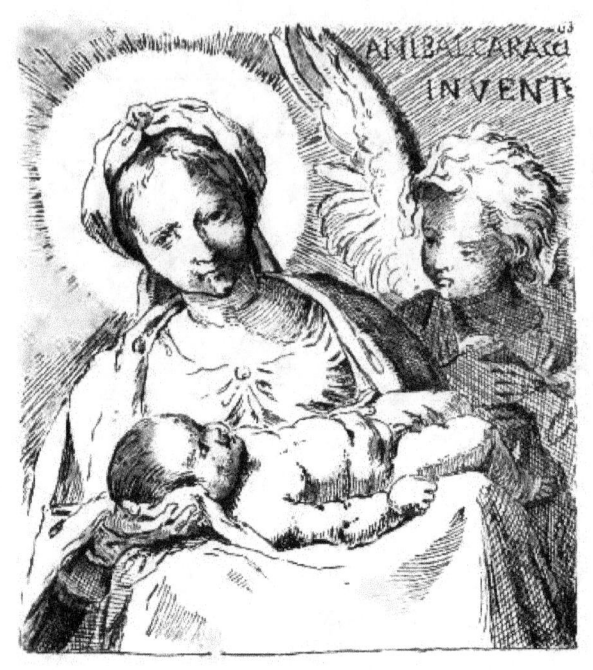

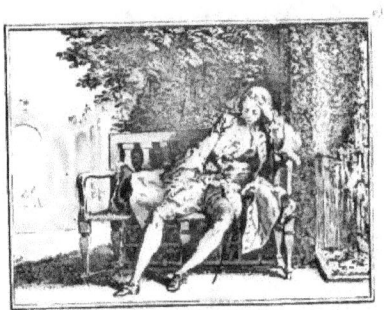

228

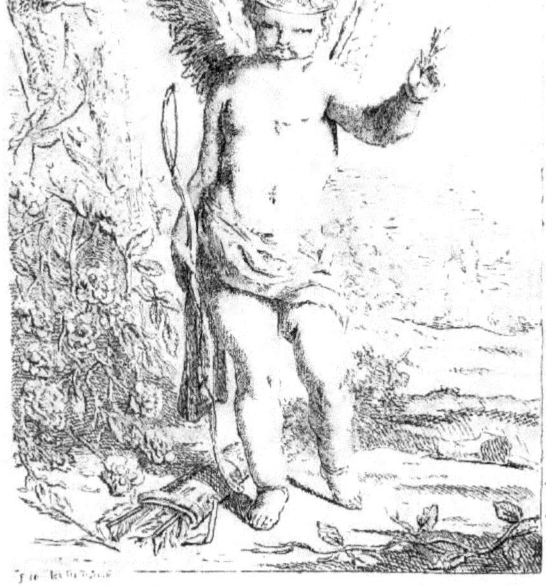

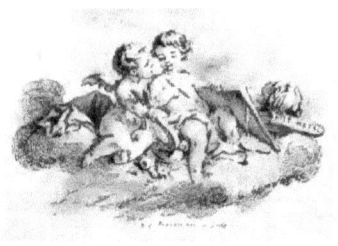

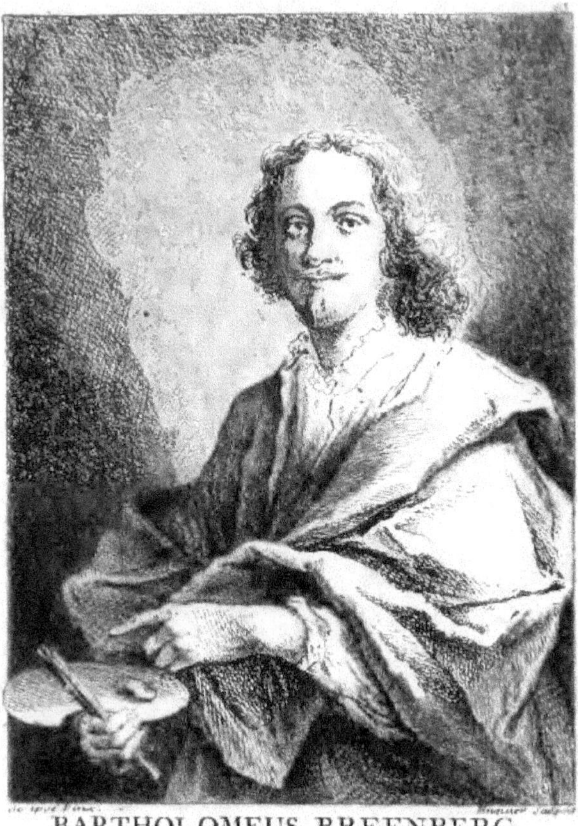

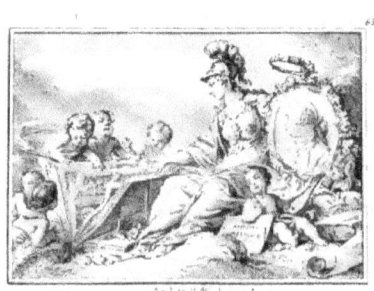

BARTHOLOMEUS BREENBERG
RURALIUM PICTOR

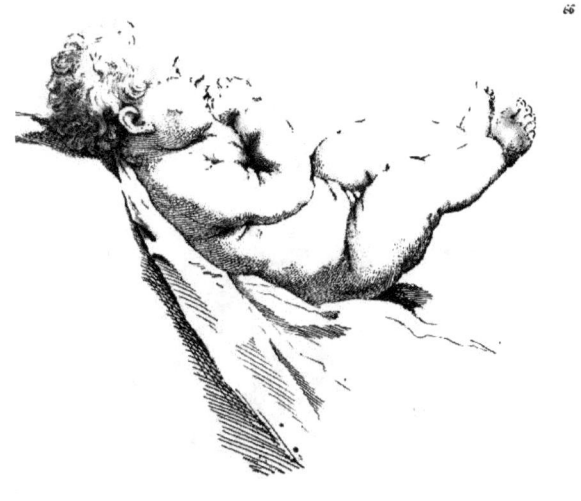

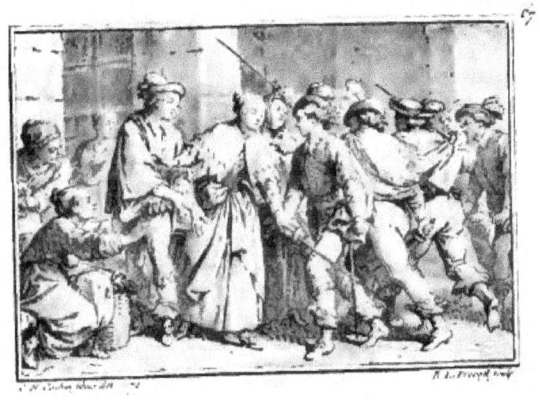

231

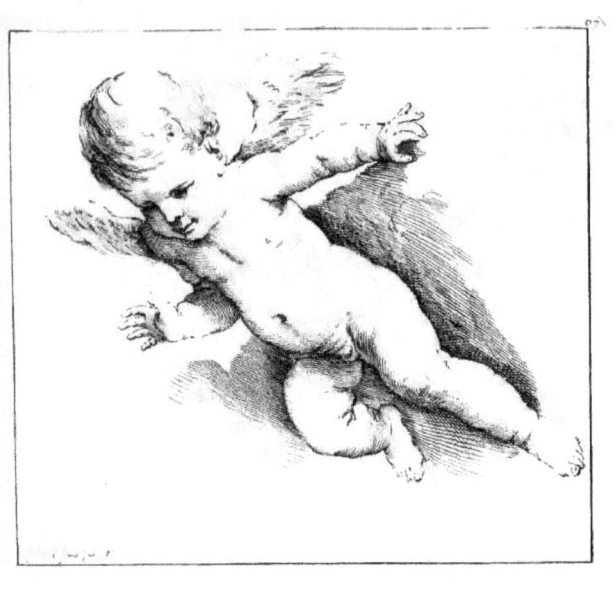

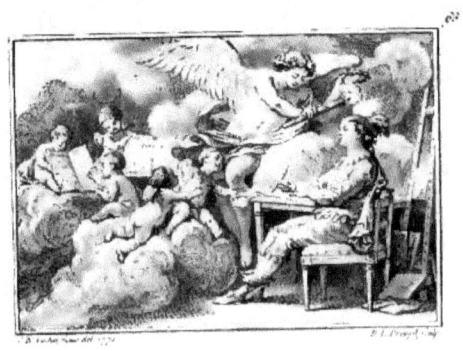

232

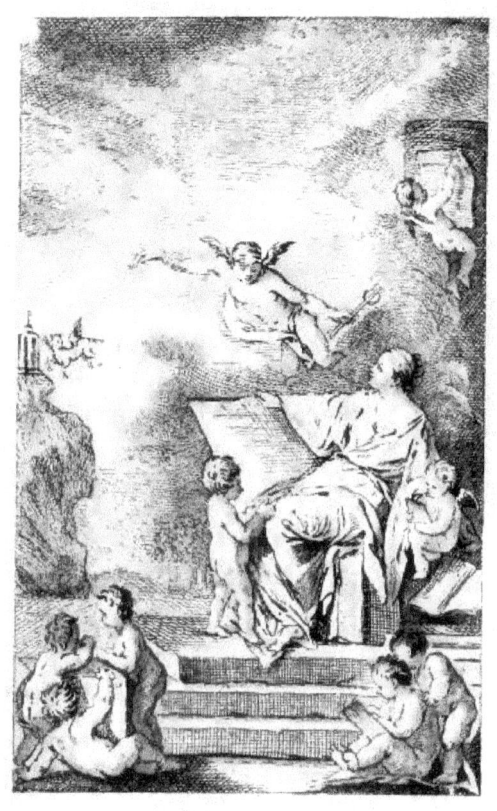

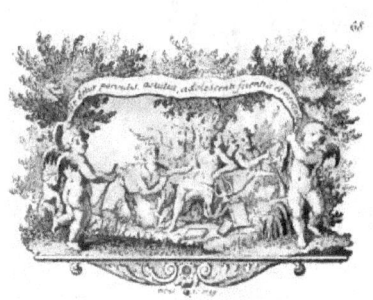

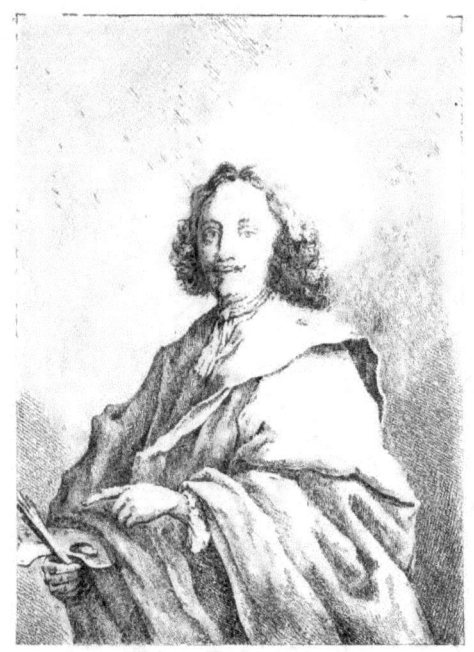

BARTOLOME BREEMBERG,

Peintre né à Utrecht en 1620. mort en 1660.

a Paris chez Huquier, rue des Mathurins

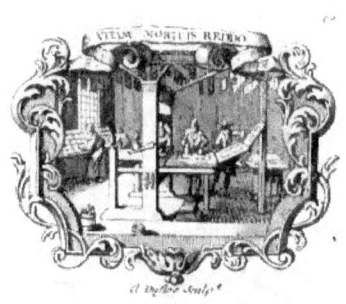

VITAM MORTIS REDDO

A. Duflos Sculp.

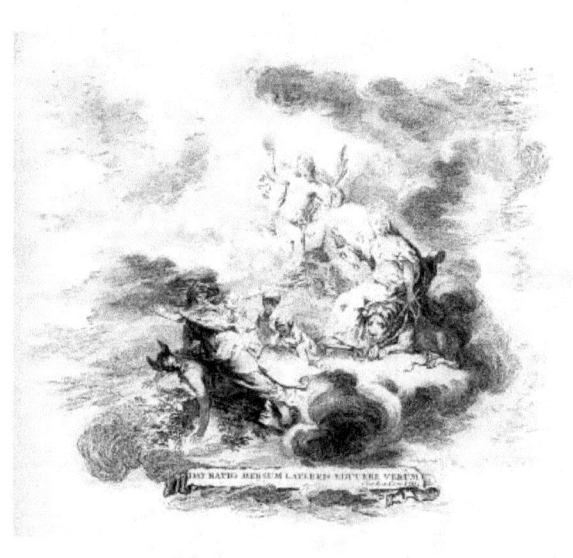

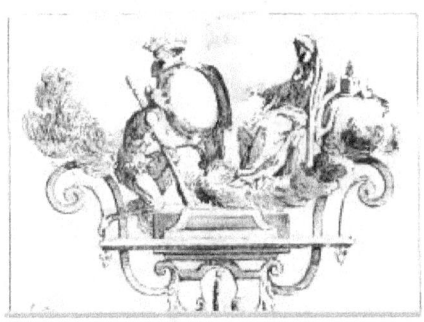

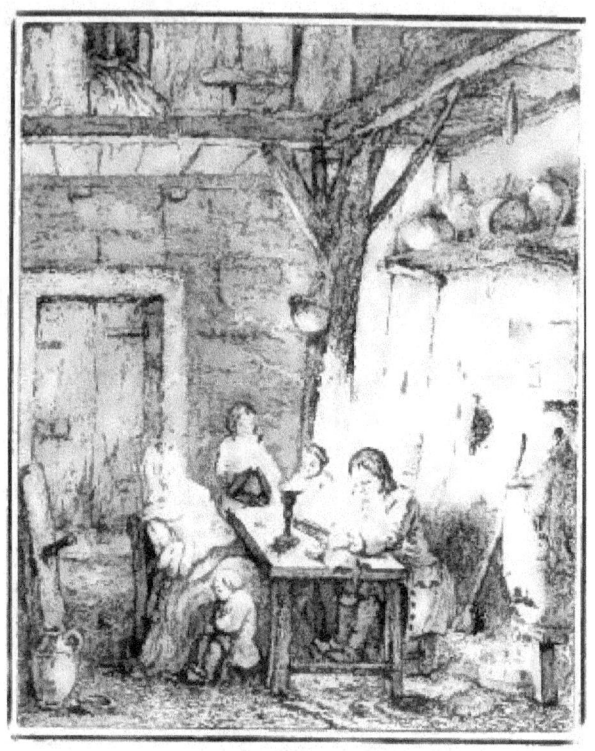

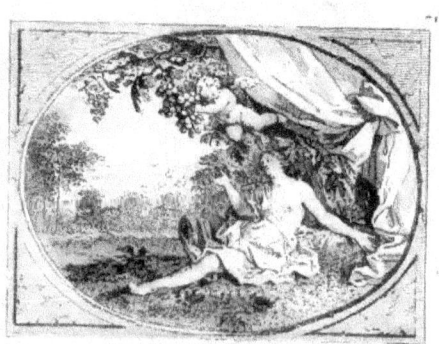

BACHUS ET ERIGONE
Gravé d'après le dessin de S.le Clere par P Avelinе .

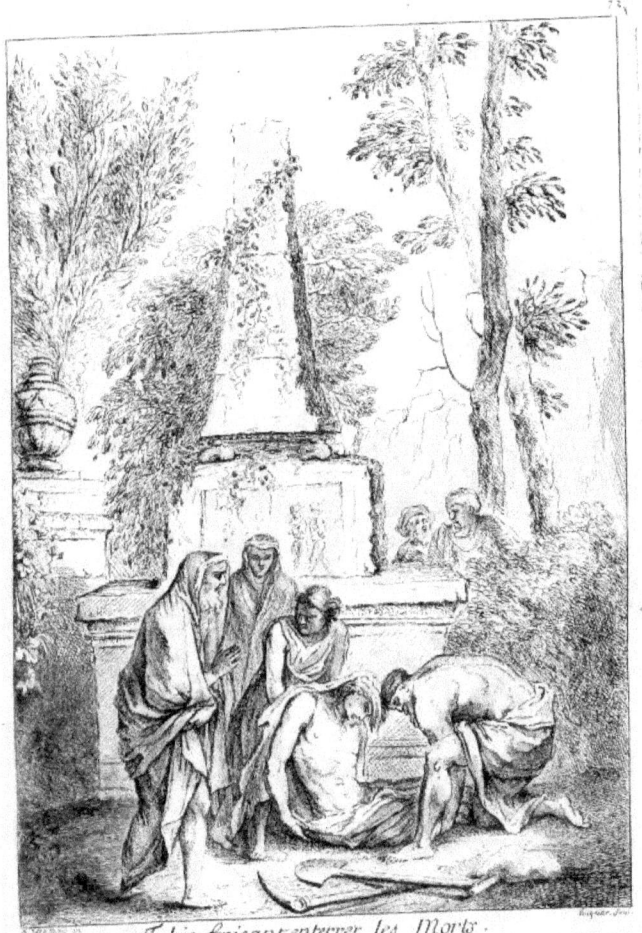

Tobie faisant enterrer les Morts.

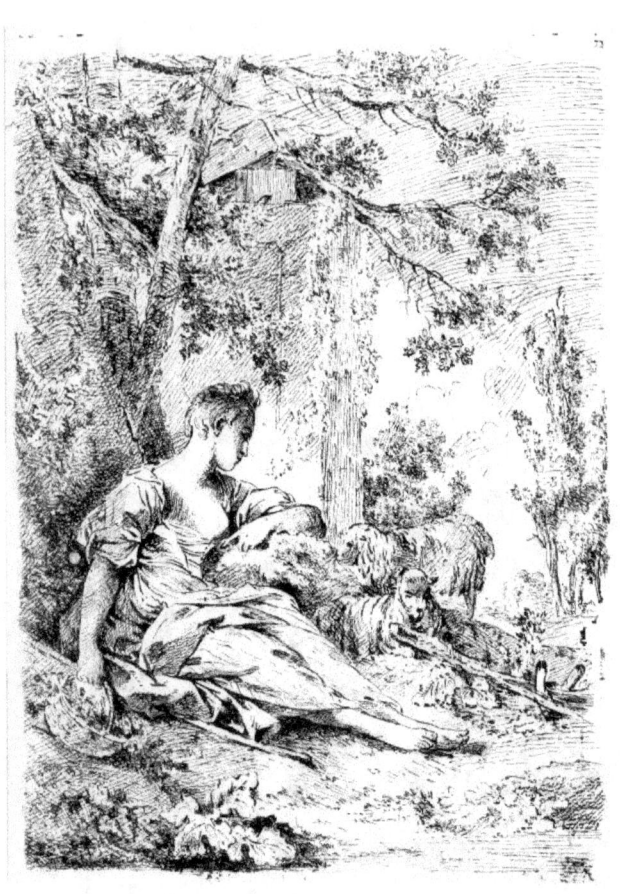

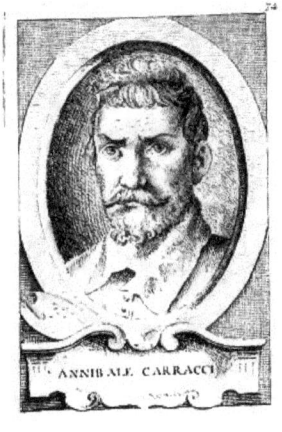

ANNIBALE CARRACCI

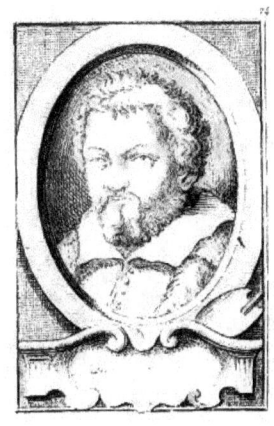

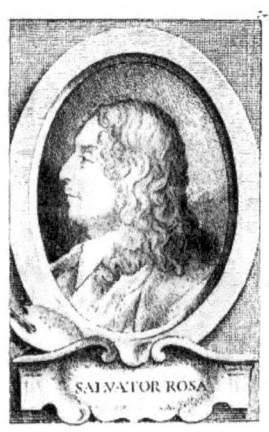

SALVATOR ROSA

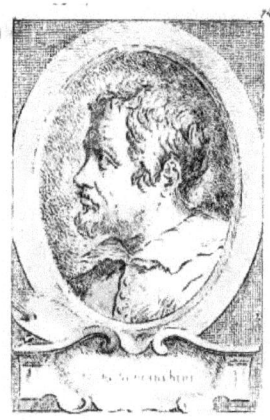

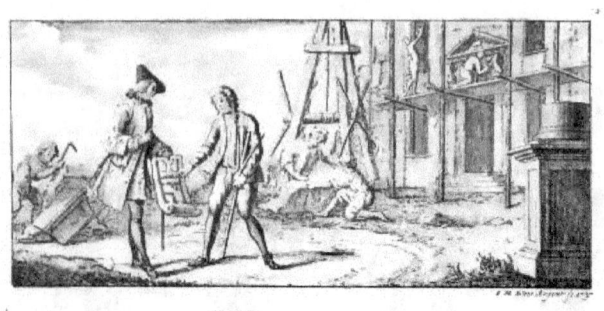

, 75

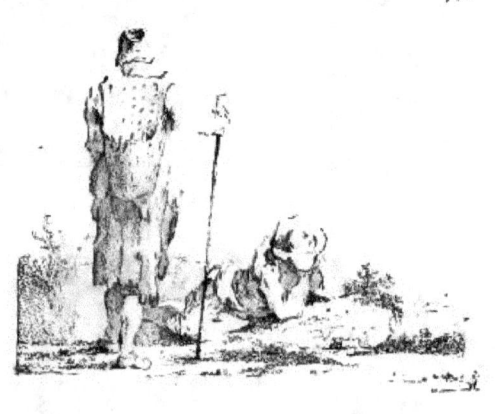

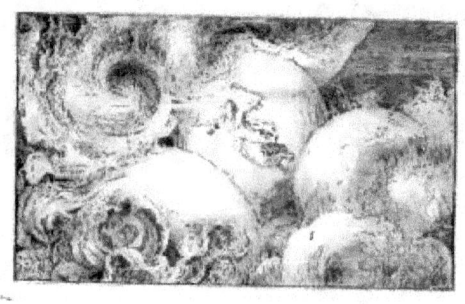

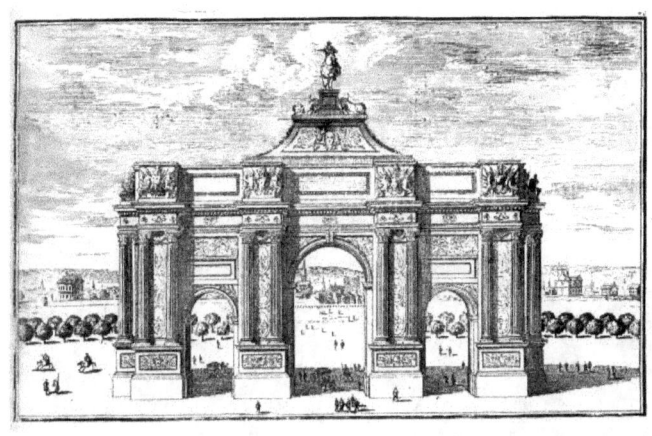

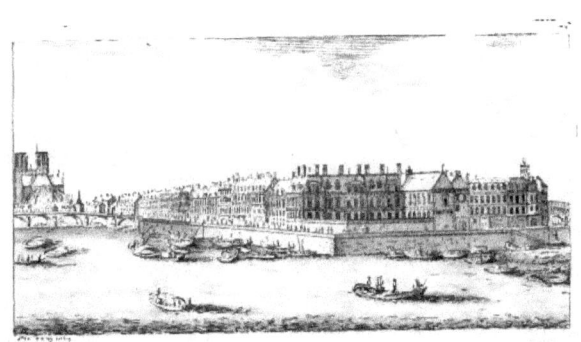

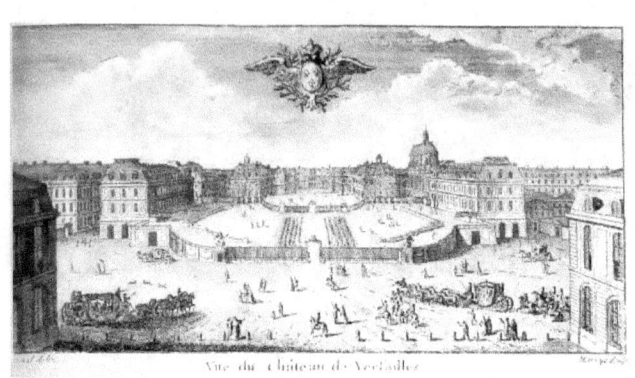

Vue du château de Versailles

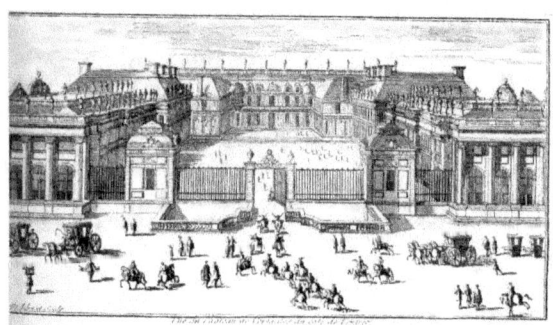

Vue du château de Versailles du coté de l'entrée

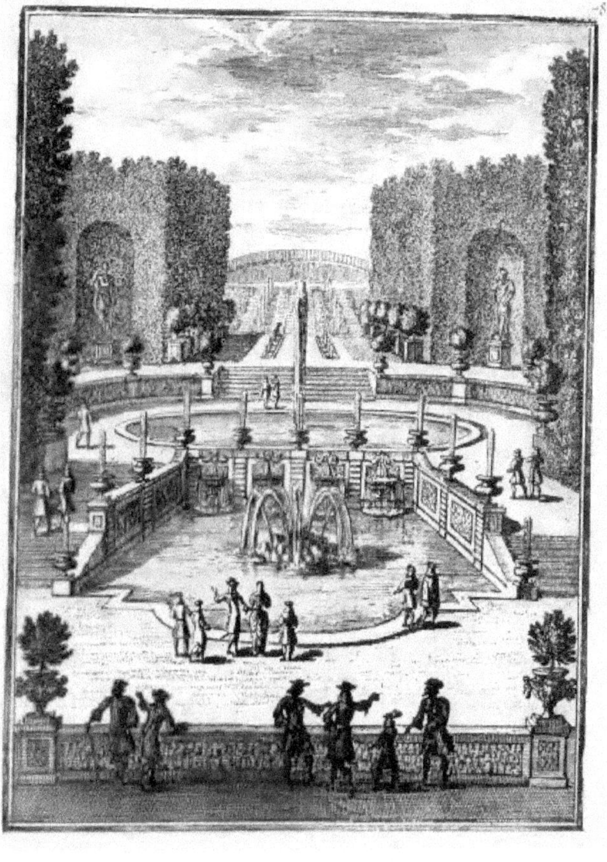

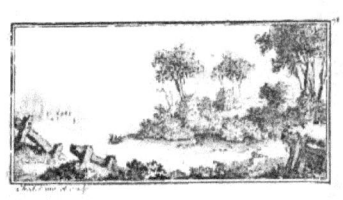

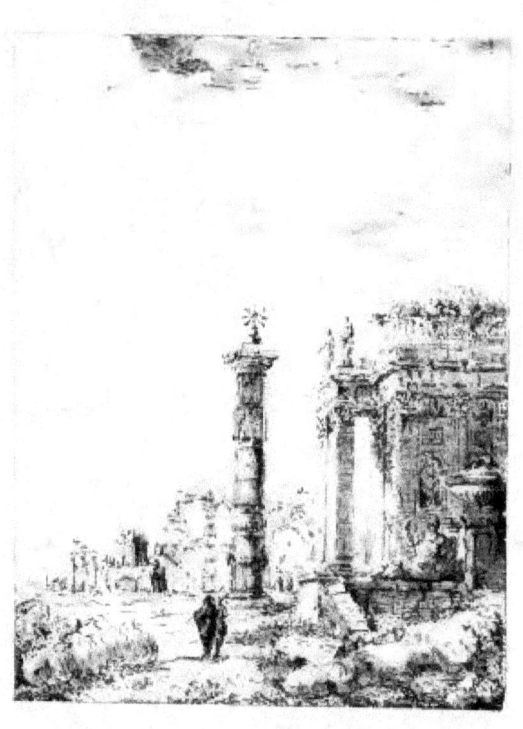

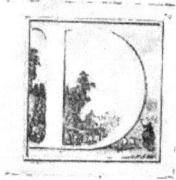 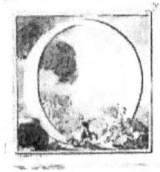

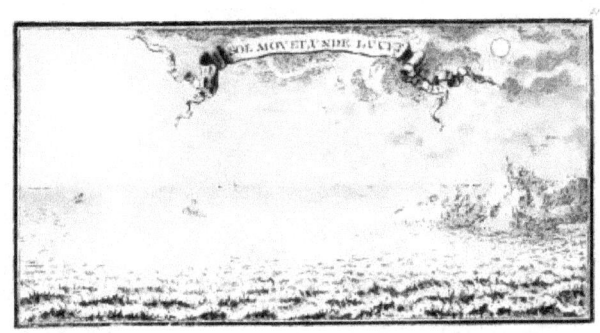

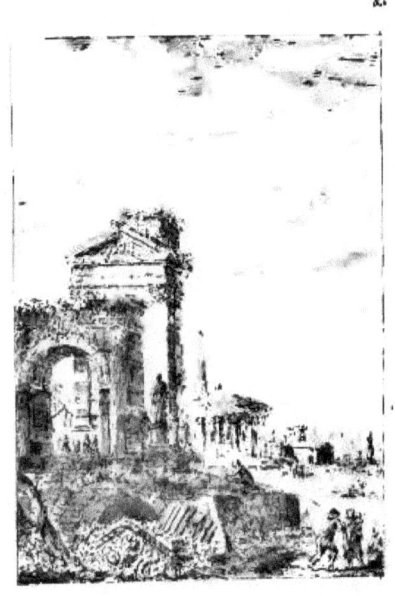

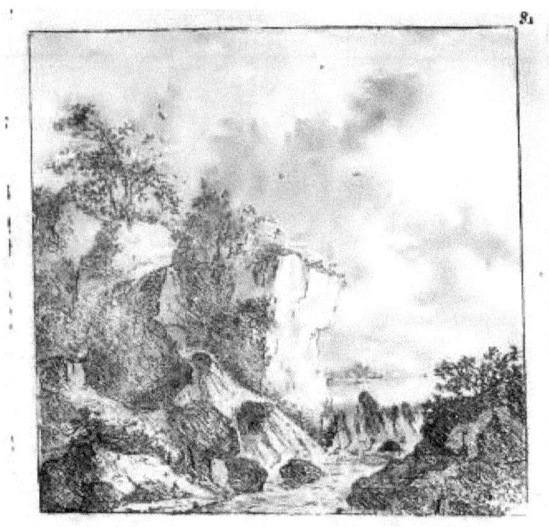

6₂

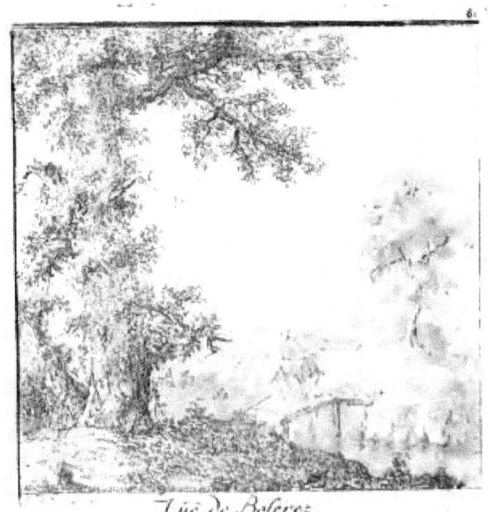

Vüe de Baferez

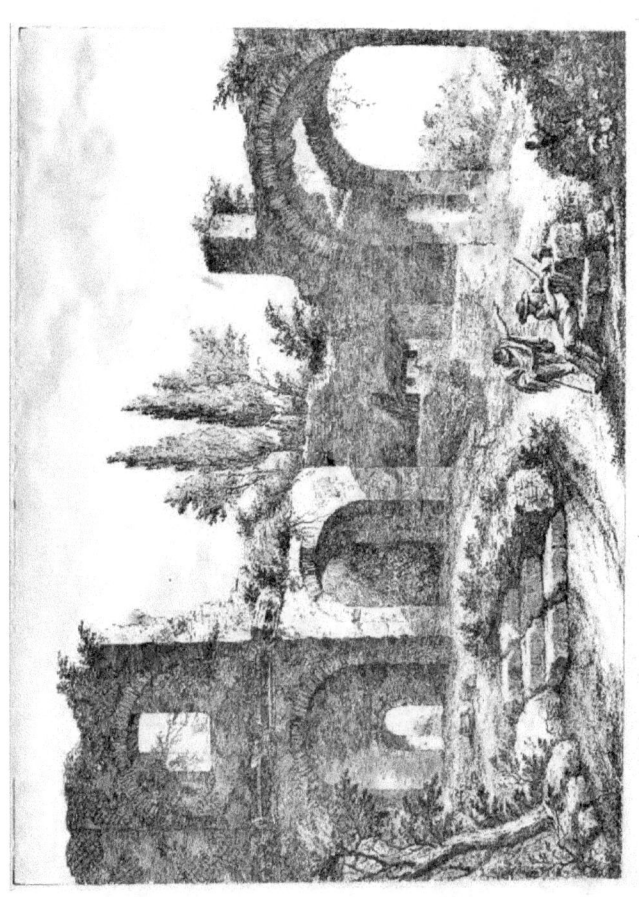

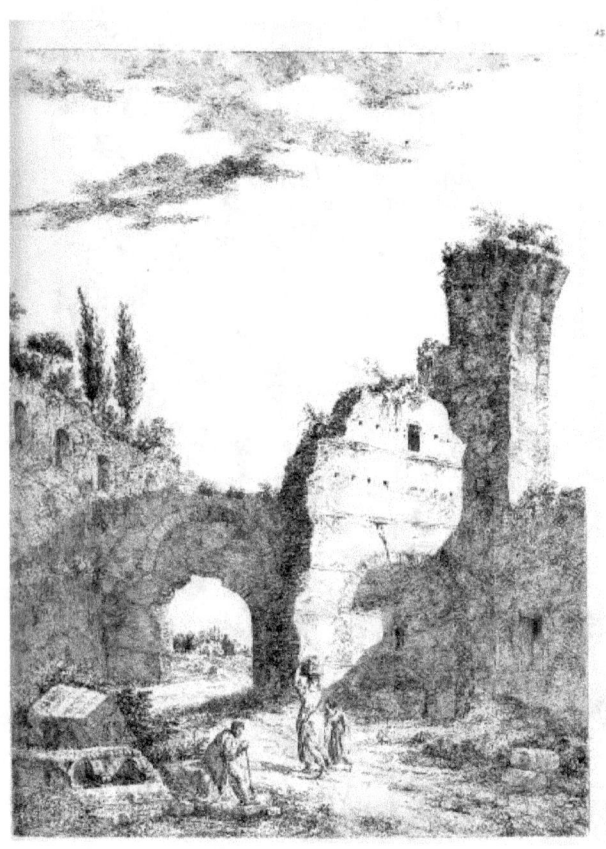

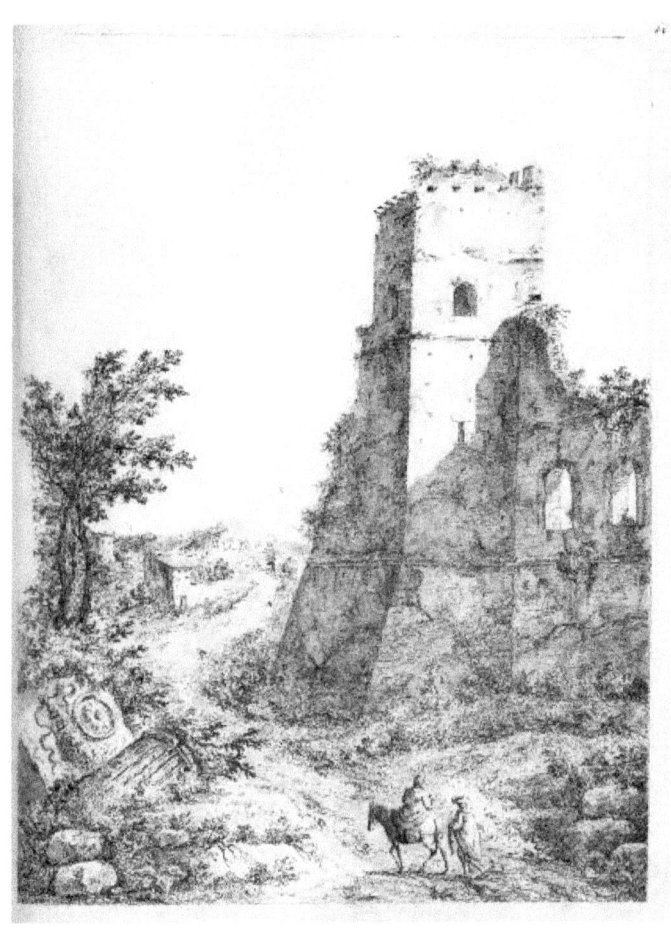

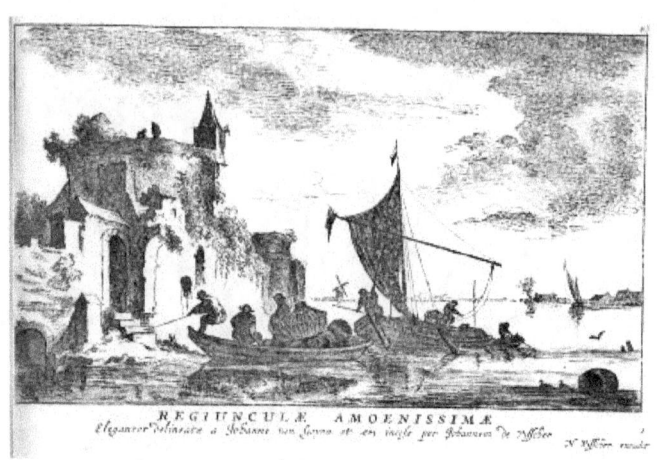

REGIUNCULÆ AMOENISSIMÆ

Eleganter delineata a Johanne van Goyen et æri incisa per Johannem de Visscher

N. Visscher excudit

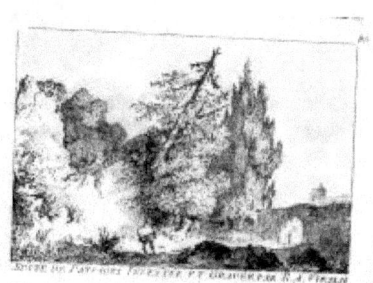

ÉTUDE DES PAYSAGES DESSINÉE ET GRAVÉE PAR R. A. VINKEL

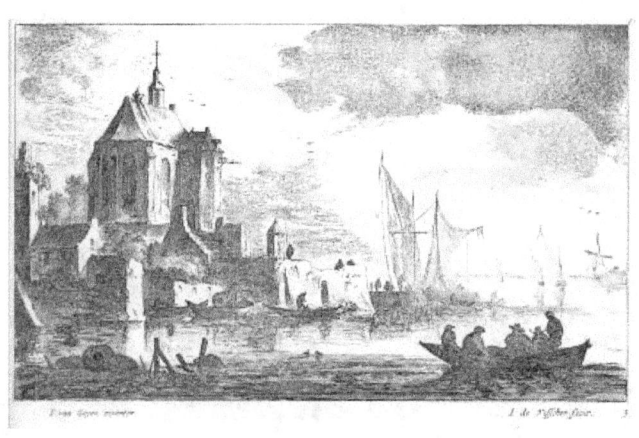

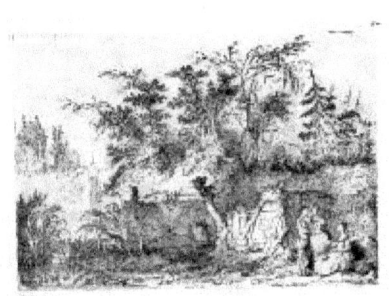

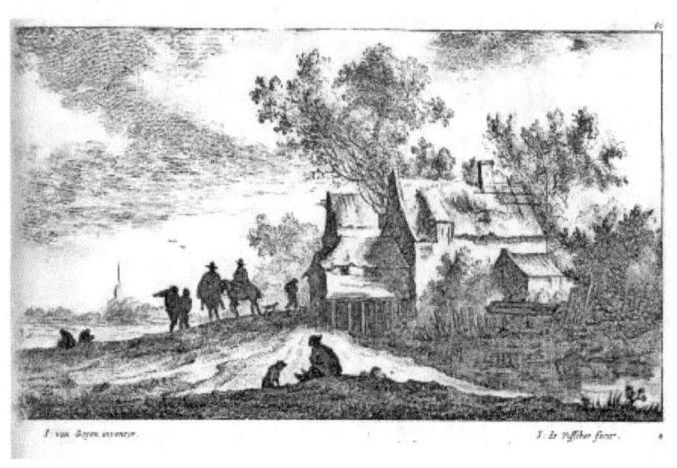

F. van Goyen inventor.　　　　　　　　　　　　J. de Vischer fecit.

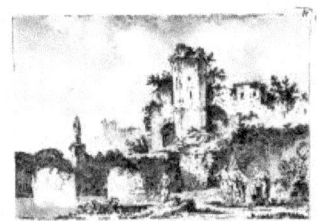

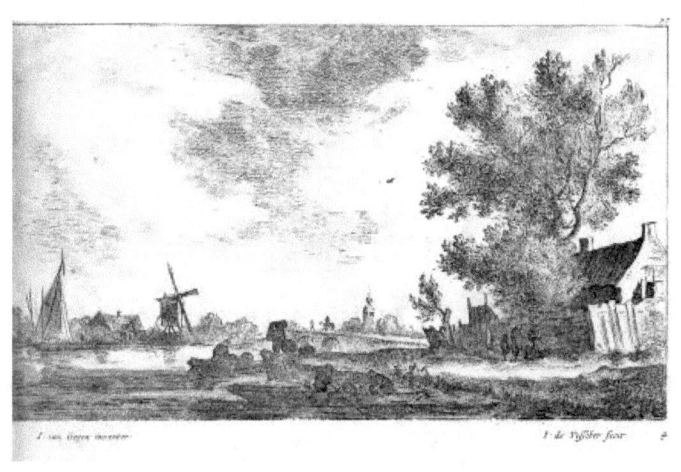

J. van Goyen inventor.   J. de Vissher fecit.

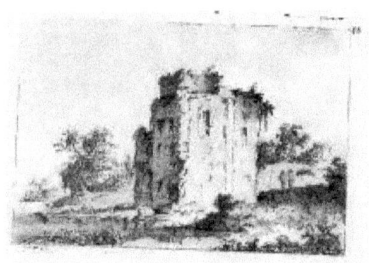

253

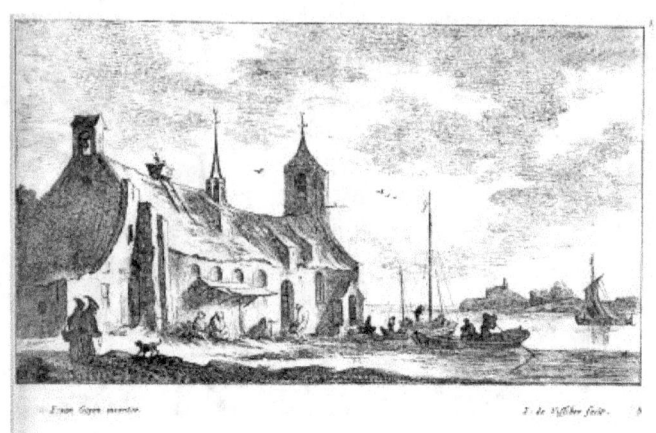

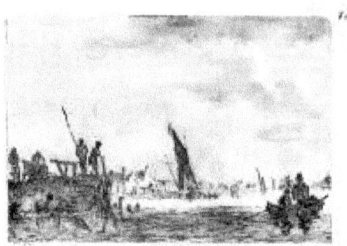

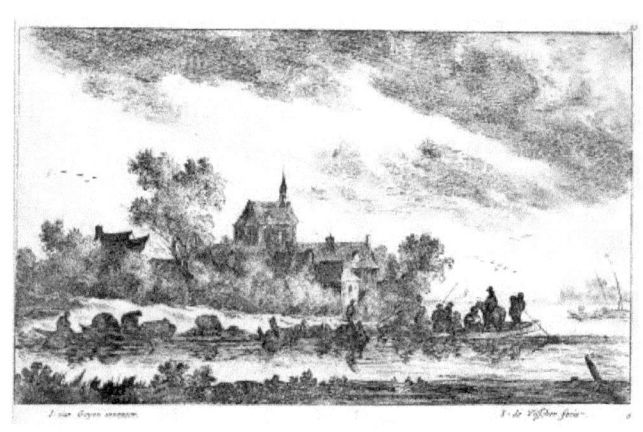

J. van Goyen inventor.   X. de Vissher fecit.

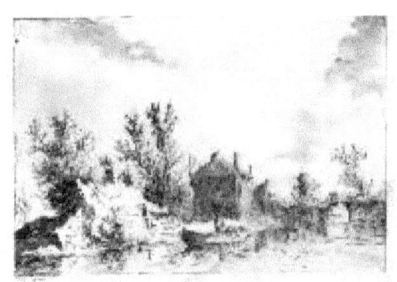

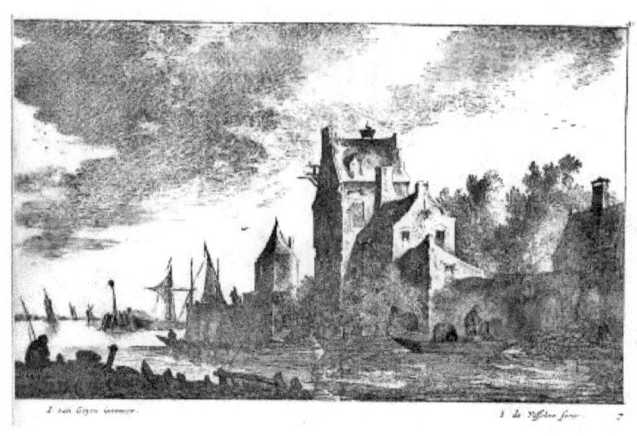

J. van Goyen invenit.   J. de Visscher fecit.   7

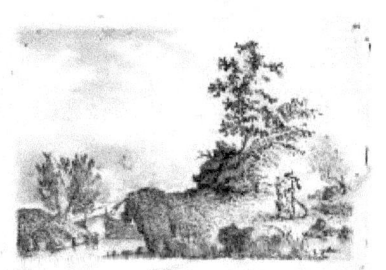

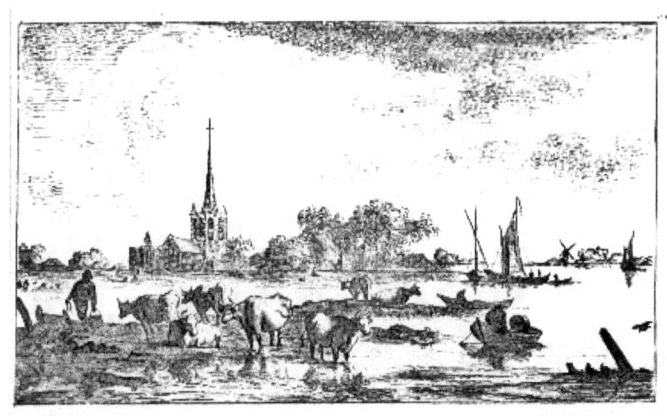

F. van Goyen inventor.   J. de Visscher fecit.

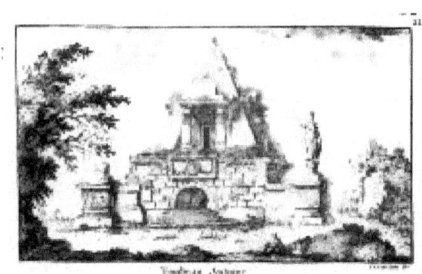

Tombeau Antique.

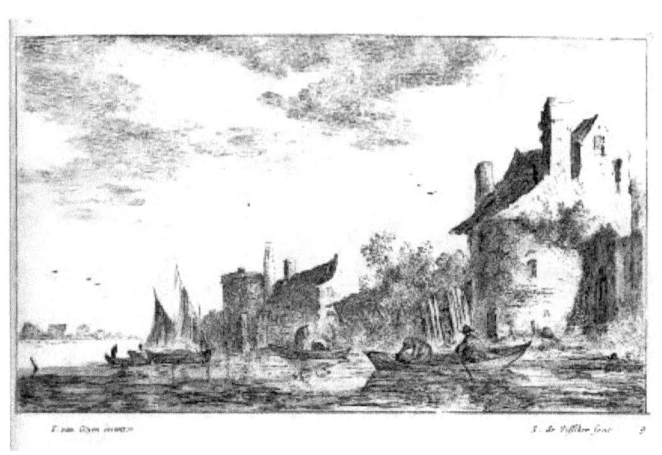

J. van Goyen inven.   S. de Vlieger fecit   9

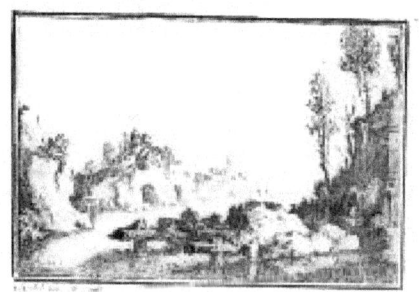

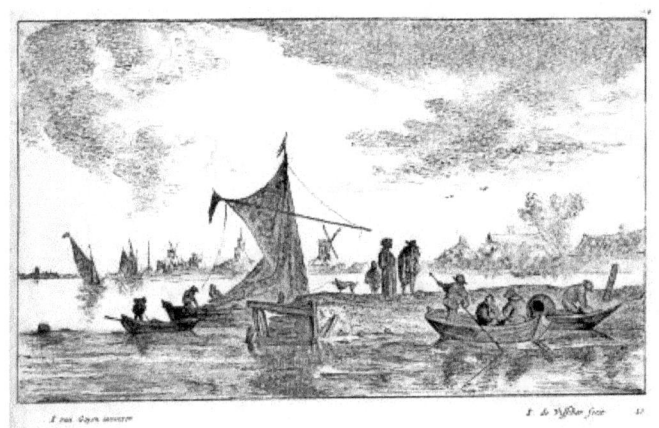

I van Goyen inventor   I de Visscher fecit   II

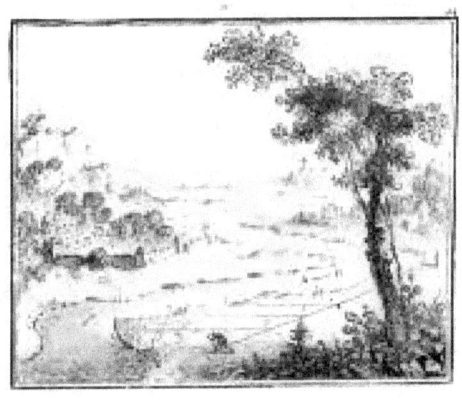

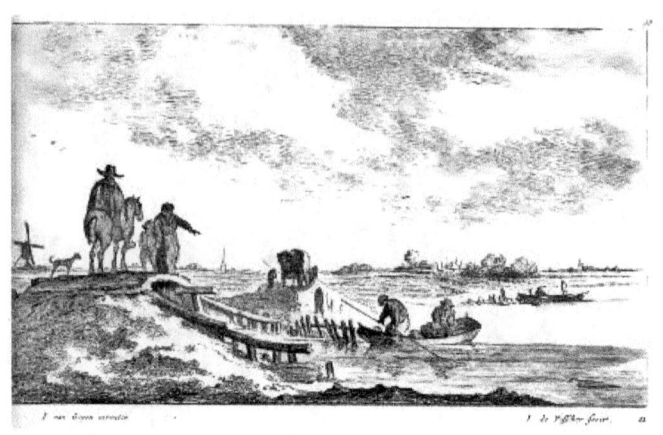

J. van Goyen invenit.   J. de Visscher fecit.   63

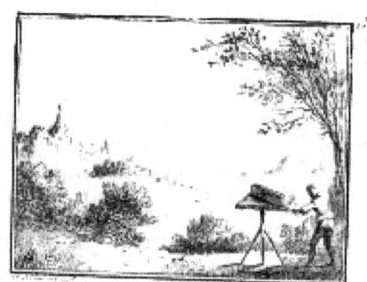

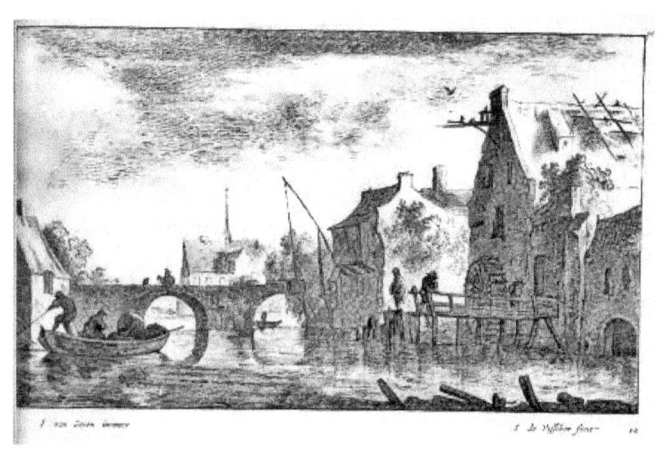

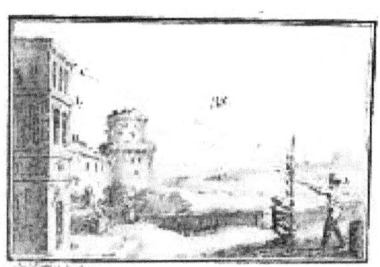

END.

Pierre Paul Ruben
Authors biograph.

Born in Cologne June 29, 1577 full high
honor of Otto Van Veen and paint coming
from Nobles parents, he was even more
illustrious by his rare talent and his deep
condition. He was sent to England in
quality of Ambassador to negotiate the
pair between this crown and that of Spain,
and was honored the Orders of Chivalry of
the Kings of France, Spain and England.
he died in Antwerp on May 1640.

Also noted: J.J. Pasquier, French
After Hubert François Bourguignon
Gravelot, French (Paris 1699 - 1773 Paris)